The Cardboard Boat Book

A Step-by-Step Instruction Manual for Building an Environmentally-Friendly 'Green' Boat with Recyclable Resources

For information and for requesting permission for quotations:

David W. Friant
PO Box 3281
Bellevue, WA
98009

www.thecardboardboatbook.com

Designed, Written, and Drawn
by
David W Friant

ISBN: 1-4392-2495-1
ISBN-13: 978-1439224953
Library of Congress Control Number: 2009900216

This book is dedicated to
my three children,
Elizabeth, Christopher,
and Caroline.
I love you lots!

 Foreward

The First Cardboard Boat Book

When I recently heard from Dave Friant after over twenty years, I was delighted to hear of his many significant life accomplishments in spite of some major obstacles. As Dave's former teacher, I was astonished to learn that a small project, which I had assigned to his Engineering Technology class over 25 years ago, had become a motivating theme through the rest of his life.

When Dave told me that he was finally going to publish the First Cardboard Boat Book, which grew out of the project, I was not surprised, remembering what a determined young man he had been. As a student I found Dave to be focused and driven to do his best. In over 30 years as a teacher of Engineering, I have rarely found a student so motivated to succeed in everything he did. When Dave asked me to write a foreword to his book, I knew he would not let go of this until it was done. Since I was partly the instigator, I felt both honored and compelled to say yes.

The cardboard boat project I assigned my Engineering Technology class in 1982 was not an original idea. I first saw the exercise while teaching in the University of Washington School of Architecture. On a small canal I watched with anticipation as students of an architecture studio launched and paddled the small boats they had designed and built out of ordinary cardboard. Some of the boats fared well and some sank immediately to the bottom of the canal.

As a teacher I have always been interested in ways of engaging students through experiential learning, but I had not thought of applying the "sink or swim" principle so literally. At the time I was teaching a course in Hydrology and Hydraulics to Dave's Civil Engineering Technology class, and I saw the cardboard boat project as a way of exploring stability and buoyancy of floating objects. So I adapted the project for our

class and the annual "Sink-R-Swim Cardboard Boat Regatta" was launched at Bellevue Community College.

Our cardboard boat project differed from the architecture project in that it focused on engineering aspects of cardboard boats. It required students to build a cardboard boat that would keep them dry while carrying them over a 100 yd. course in a small lake near campus. Students were allowed a limited quantity of cardboard, tape and glue. The projects were evaluated on their stability, buoyancy, maneuverability, and durability during the contest. We even had boat races to see which boat was the fastest.

The project began with design sketches, following the engineering principles students were learning. Next was a testing phase, where students built a small scale model of their boats and tested them with model weights in a water tank in our lab. I clearly remember coming into the lab one day to find Dave suspended in air, balancing on the backs of two chairs. When I asked what he was doing, he said he was trying to find his center of gravity. I was impressed to see how seriously Dave was taking this exercise. Of course his motivation and competitive spirit were infecting the rest of the class and I knew then what a great learning experience this would be for all of us.

The next phase was the actual construction where students worked out the details of strength, stability, and stiffness of the boats and worked on jointing and waterproofing their crafts. In the regatta, Dave's original cardboard boat was a head turner, and glided like a water bug across the lake, easily winning in every category. The boat design, craftsmanship, and performance were exceptional. Dave incorporated everything he had learned in class and moved so far beyond with a project that had taken on a life of its own.

Dave had succeeded in building not just any

cardboard boat; Dave's boat was "**THE**" cardboard boat, and everyone who saw it, knew it.

An important development in the cardboard boat book was the introduction of Computer Aided Drafting and Design (CADD) to our curriculum while Dave was a student. Along with a consortium of colleges our program was granted funding to implement CADD with some of the first personal computers in the college. In a lab we installed 3D CADD software on six new PC's, where I introduced students to Computer Aided Design.

Captivated by the power of this new technology, Dave Friant immersed himself in the study of CADD the following summer, motivated by the desire to illustrate the great cardboard boat designs he had developed. Dave learned CADD so well he began teaching it to others. The amazingly detailed and clear fold-out illustrations in this book are the result of Dave's mastery of CADD.

The boat designs in this book are based in sound engineering principles, and excellent craftsmanship through careful construction and testing. With the help of clear illustrations and concise but thorough instructions they are easy to build successfully. Like the project that generated them and the dream of Dave Friant that has sustained them, they have been proven over many years to be strong and durable.

I am deeply honored to commend this book to anyone who wants to build an inexpensive and small boat. By following Dave's excellent guidance in the book I'm sure you will feel a sense of accomplishment in building something useful and enjoyable.

I congratulate Dave on his many accomplishments but especially on the completion of his long term vision to produce an excellent "How-To" book on building cardboard boats. The boats and the book about them are testament to the learning and satisfaction that comes when a person applies himself fully to something about which he is passionate. Dave's original cardboard boats were

designed and built with much more than cardboard and glue. The most important components were passion, hard work, focus and follow-through. I am convinced that if you bring a little of these magic ingredients to your first cardboard boat, it will carry you easily and far across the water.

Michael F. Hein, P.E., Professor
McWorter School of Building Science
Auburn University

Jan. 1, 2009

B.C.C.   ENGRT 266   HYDRAULICS

THE FIRST ANNUAL ENGINEERING TECH.

'SINK-R-SWIM' REGATTA

This project is designed to test your understanding of the principles of bouyancy and stability of floating objects.

You are required to construct a boat of ⅛" thick corrugated cardboard. Keeping in mind that the proof of the product is in the paddling, you will test your craft on a 100 yd. course along the shores of Lake Sammamish, Thursday afternoon, June 2.

REQUIREMENTS

* 36 SF MAXIMUM, CARDBOARD PER PERSON

* All SOLID CONSTRUCTION, ⅛" SINGLE-PLY CORRUGATED CARDBOARD

* NO OTHER INITIALLY SOLID MATERIALS MAY BE USED, LIQUIDS SUCH AS PAINTS AND GLUES & WAXES ARE YOUR ONLY ALLIES.

* A ¹⁄₁₂ SCALE MODEL (36 sq.in.) MUST BE BUILT OF LIGHTER WEIGHT CARDBOARD AND TESTED IN THE LAB. ON THURSDAY, MAY 5.

* 100 yds. OF PADDLED SELF PROPULSION ACROSS LAKE SAMMAMISH - PADDLE MUST BE CONFIGURED FROM CORRUGATED CARDBOARD, NOT FROM INITIAL 36 SF.

* ONE BEVERAGE HOLDER MUST BE CAST INTEGRALLY INTO BOAT FROM CORRUGATED CARDBOARD. (PADDLING IN JUNE CAN BE THIRSTY WORK!)

— GOOD LUCK & HAPPY BOATING! —

Professor Hein Engineering Assignment - 1982

Preface

The Story of The Cardboard Boat Book

For every book that has ever been written there is a story that goes along with it. The story is usually bigger than the book as the book is the culmination of the story that drove the creation of the book in the first place. *The Cardboard Boat Book* is such a book and its story spans an entire career and a lifetime pursuit to complete a project that began twenty-five years ago. The story involves a dream, as well as a belief that these boats are truly seaworthy, and a desire to provide the world with something that has not yet been done like this before.

You are now holding the completion of the story, *The Cardboard Boat Book*. This is a story of a college physics project that so engrossed my mind and soul that it has followed me throughout my entire career beginning with my first job in the computer industry. The story continued as I started my own computer company and shut down my company, through marriage, divorce, and raising children, including heartbreaks as well as great joy along the way. It has followed me as I traveled all over the world working for some of the most interesting and successful companies of the 21st century. *The Cardboard Boat Book* has opened doors for me for 25 years. Who could have known that a college physics project and a cardboard boat would have done so much for one person? It is a story of dedication and perseverance to develop a simple solution for an intriguing problem. The boats themselves are an elegant, simple, and clever design, crafted from an unconventional boat building material.

In the beginning of this project the personal computer as we know it today did not exist. We used calculators, descriptive geometry, algebra, and trigonometry to design our ideas and put them on paper. The cardboard boat designs in this book were a product of those simpler times. After lots of testing on paper and in the classroom the design

worked! It not only worked, it worked really well. I then expounded on the original idea and built them larger and stronger. Then one day I had the vision of *The Cardboard Boat Book*, something that just happened due to all of the time and effort put into the project.

I first proposed the idea of writing the book to my engineering professor. I envisioned the book being a college assignment to satisfy my elective credit requirements. He agreed to my proposal and I subsequently earned 15 'A' credits for writing the book which allowed me to graduate with honors. This was the first success, or as I like to refer to it, Chapter one of *The Cardboard Boat Book*. Little did I know at the time that this was the first of many chapters to come over the span of 25 years.

Chapter two: I consulted with my technical writing professor as I wrote the book. Along the way she introduced me to a professional editor. The editor took such a liking to this idea that she brought it to the attention of a few publishers she knew. This exposure led to signing a contract with a publisher in Canada. This was another big win for *The Cardboard Boat Book*, but with this win came a new predicament. I was required to spend thousands of dollars to have the technical drawings professionally drafted for the publisher. As a young college kid I had no money to speak of except what was currently in my bank account and that would be gone in less than 2 weeks.

Chapter three: It was at this time that the college purchased a number of new computers for the engineering program. The computers were an early predecessor to the IBM PC. They were specifically configured for one purpose, to perform computer-assisted-drafting. The configuration included a 3-Dimensional drafting program running on an S-100 Bus, Seattle Computing Products DOS, a Visual 500 terminal, two 360k floppy disk drives and a small HP Plotter. I had an idea. Here was my solution. I am an engineer, and I could draw my own drawings with this computer. I could draft the drawings without paying someone to do it for me and I could learn how to use a computer at the same time. Little did I know that this would change my life forever and I would spend the next 25 years of my career in the computer industry from this day forward.

Chapter four: It just so happened that the college purchased the computers a month before the summer school break in 1983. I proposed to my professor that I use the computers over the summer to draft the drawings for *The Cardboard Boat Book*. My professor thought about it for a few minutes and then handed me the key to the computer lab and said, "I am going on summer vacation, teach me what you learn when I get back, see ya!" That was all I needed to get started. I barely knew how to turn on the computer let alone use it productively. Another thing, there wasn't much documentation to even help me make sense of this thing. Did that stop me? No way! I had a vision and I kept moving forward. I proceeded to spend the entire summer working in the computer lab all day, every day, day after day. When I learned how to do something I would document it. I spoke with the author of the software on an almost daily basis. I spent hours drafting the drawings for *The Cardboard Boat Book* and I learned everything about that early computer that I could, not for the sake of the computer but for the sake of drafting the drawings for *The Cardboard Boat Book*.

Chapter five: Once summer was over and my professor returned from vacation he was pleased with the progress that I had made. The opportunities were now just beginning. Based on my new experience I found myself lecturing my own engineering class and managing the computer lab that school year under the supervision of my engineering professor. The college got word that a student was lecturing his own class and soon approached me and asked if I was interested in teaching a class in the evenings to practicing professionals on how to use the computer system. Of course I said yes and a new chapter of *The Cardboard Boat Book* was in the works.

Chapter six: After a few quarters of teaching classes for the college the next opportunity presented itself. I was recruited by a local start-up computer company to teach their customers how to use the CAD systems they were selling and also to assist their computer sales people by demonstrating the technology. I jumped on this like everything before it. Soon I found myself sought after as an instructor and a consultant in a fledgling industry surrounding the personal computer. Once again the plot thickened. I was recruited by a second start-up company to sell CAD workstations. The last thing I wanted to do was be a salesman. To make a long story short, after 5 years as the top salesman for this company the company was sold, their business plan shifted, and I began looking for my next opportunity.

What happened to The Cardboard Boat Book in all of this? Well, the publisher in Canada went out of business before the book was published and they returned the manuscript and the drawings to me. I was saddened but I was so busy working with computers and learning about many different types of businesses and manufacturing processes that I soon forgot about the book. Sadly it ended up in a box in my attic with all the memorabilia surrounding the project.

Chapter seven: After 12 years of gaining experience in the computer business I was one of the successful computer 'geeks' in the Pacific Northwest. The original computer system I used eventually morphed into the IBM PC®, the XT®, the AT®, the 386, the 486 and beyond. Over the years MS-DOS®, and then Windows®, and Microsoft® grew up in my backyard. I eventually opened my own company selling CAD/CAM workstations and services to the top manufacturing companies in the Pacific Northwest.

Three more years went by and I began to wonder where had the time gone. After my first marriage ended I shut my company down and got a real job and struggled as a single parent for a number of years. Once again *The Cardboard Boat Book* facilitated the next step in my career. I had now gained so much practical experience working with computers that I landed a Senior position with a leading global technology corporation and wound up traveling all over the world implementing biometric identification projects for national governments, law enforcement agencies, and large-scale commercial implementations of their technology. This chapter in my story lasted for 10 years when I once again shifted gears and decided I wanted to work for the big company itself, Microsoft®, which is where I am at the time this book is published.

Chapter eight: Around 2007 something began to happen to me. I woke up one day and realized how much time had passed and how fast life had moved along. I began to do some soul searching and realized I missed what got me here in the first place, *The Cardboard Boat Book*. My second wife, who is the love and joy of my life, began to suggest that I dust off the book and publish it. After all, the book is one of those things that I had never completed and it meant so much to me. Why did I ever stop working on it? Simple, life got in the way and the book got put on the back burner. That was until now, until I was ready for it again, and until the software tools that are necessary to do it right were available, and until the world was ready for an environmentally-friendly 'green' boat. I began to think the time was right, the time is now.

Chapter nine: I pulled out my original manuscript, the computer drawings, and all the old memorabilia. I updated my page layout software, my technical illustration software, developed a simple web site, and buckled down once again and learned how to use new software tools to begin the process of re-writing the book. I ran into challenges such as, the old CAD drawing database was so outdated I had to jump through hoops to convert the old data into a format I could use. Some drawings had to be completely re-drawn. I rallied all my resources together and with a new vision for an old idea I diligently worked to reproduce the book.

Chapter ten: You are holding in your hands *The Cardboard Boat Book*, the book that created a lifetime career for one person. It is a story of dedication and perseverance to complete a project that began 25 years ago. It is now available to everyone in the world who wants to build their own environmentally-friendly boat from recyclable resources.

I believe there isn't anything half as much fun as messing around in a boat on a sunny day. *The Cardboard Boat Book* teaches you how to build your own boat for the price of the paint, glue, and tape required to put it together, it doesn't harm the environment, and it is fully recyclable.

I am very proud to say with a smile on my face that "I finally wrote *The Cardboard Boat Book*!" I hope you have fun with this book and your boat. I also want to encourage you to follow your dreams, you never know what may come of them.

~Dave Friant

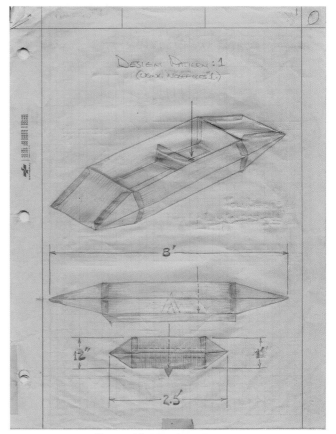

Cardboard boat drawing - 1982

Acknowledgements

When you invest the time and energy to follow through and achieve the completion of a personal dream you realize that you would not have been able to do it without the support of many people. Some people inspired you, some people performed hands-on activities, some people provided resources, some people dreamed with you, and everyone cheered you on.

This project is that type of dream. It has consumed my entire mind and soul for more years than I care to remember. From the first time my Engineering Professor, Michael Hein, challenged me with the idea of designing and building boats with cardboard I have spent countless hours, days, and nights, dreaming of how to design a successful and viable boat from a material that is made from paper. This book is the culmination of that dream.

Although I have designed a number of cardboard boats, the boat in this book is my all time favorite, it is my original design, and it is a marvel of simplicity and engineering excellence.

My very dependable lifelong friend and colleague, Jeff Ridley, spent countless hours and energy assisting in the construction of the boats, hauling the boats to and from the water, putting up with all the tests I put the boats through to determine their strength and seaworthiness, and listening to me tell him for years that I was really going to write this book. Without his support and commitment this book would not exist.

Another lifelong friend, Jeff James, consulted with me on the use of computers in the early days while writing the book. My friend and colleague Jim Merrick spent many hours teaching me how to use the CAD system. The author of the CAD software, Steve Ford, was extremely responsive and supportive to me while I was learning how to use his software. My friend and colleague Mark Sanders donated his time and photographic expertise. My Brother Joel spent a lot of energy convincing me to write this book. My Brother Andy provided me with the supplies to draw the original drawings on paper. My Father and Stepmother provided photography equipment and provided the typewriter I used to write the original draft. My Mother believed in the boats from the very beginning and encouraged me at all times. My Technical Writing Professor, Linda Leeds, helped me express my thoughts in words and edited the original manuscript. I must also mention Larry Steckler. Larry is a man who has spent his entire life in the publishing business and was instrumental in assisting my efforts to finally publish the book.

Lastly, I want to thank my wonderful wife. She is the person who has completed my life and is my inspiration and best friend. She convinced me to buckle down and do this for me. I would not have finished the book without her encouragement, dedication, and patience.

The people mentioned here are a few of the many people who listened to me talk about *The Cardboard Boat Book* for many years. A lot of people, all shapes and sizes, have been recruited to test the boats for seaworthiness.

I want to thank all of the people that have touched this project along the way for their support. For all of their waiting and listening to me I am very happy to say, '**I finally wrote *The Cardboard Boat Book*!**'

I hope everyone that builds a cardboard boat finds the enjoyment that I have found over the years messing around in my cardboard boats.

Disclaimer

David W. Friant is the Designer of the cardboard boats and Author of *The Cardboard Boat Book*. Herein after referred to as the Designer/Author. The cardboard boats are an experimental watercraft for Homebuilder construction. The Homebuilder intends to build a cardboard boat from *The Cardboard Boat Book* and understands and agrees to the following terms, conditions, and requirements.

Boat Design Integrity

The Homebuilder understands and agrees that many factors affect the design integrity of the cardboard boats, including the design requirements for materials, the design requirements for stability and center of gravity, and the requirements for water damage protection.

The Homebuilder agrees to construct the cardboard boats according to the instructions in this book. The Homebuilder agrees not to make any modification or substitution of any component part of the cardboard boats.

The Designer/Author reserves the right to make recommended revisions in the plans and construction of the boats at any time without liability to the Designer/Author, as such revisions or changes may be deemed advisable from time to time.

Liability

The Homebuilder understands and agrees that many factors beyond the control of the Designer/Author significantly affect the operational safety of the cardboard boats constructed by him or her. Factors include the quality of the boats as constructed by The Homebuilder or others, the performance by The Homebuilder or others of maintenance procedures and repairs, or the operation of the boats by The Homebuilder or others. The Homebuilder also understands and agrees that the construction, maintenance, and/or repair of any cardboard boat may involve the use of tools, equipment, and construction methods which may present safety hazards which are beyond the control of the Designer/Author. The Designer/Author does not warrant the integrity of the cardboard used to build a cardboard boat. The Homebuilder agrees to inspect all materials used in construction prior to assembly for structural integrity and damage.

The Homebuilder accepts sole responsibility for the construction and operation of the boats constructed by him or her, and The Homebuilder releases the Designer /Author from any liability for any bodily injury or property damage arising from his or her construction, maintenance, or operation of any cardboard boat. The Homebuilder understands that the cost of the boat designs and *The Cardboard Boat Book* would be substantially higher should such waiver of liability not be made.

The entire risk as to the quality and performance of the boats is with the The Homebuilder. *The Cardboard Boat Book* is provided "as is" without expressed or implied warranty of any kind, including the implied warranties of merchantability and fitness for a particular purpose. Should the cardboard boats prove defective, the The Homebuilder (not the Designer/Author) assumes the entire cost of all necessary repair or correction.

Always wear a Personal-Flotation-Device when in or around water.

Table of Contents

What is a Cardboard Boat?

A cardboard boat is a lightweight 'environmentally-friendly' boat constructed with 1/4-inch thick, 275-pound test, double-wall corrugated cardboard. The boats simply fold up from cardboard obtaining their strength from the geometry of the component parts. The boats are eight-feet long, weigh about 25-pounds, and can safely accommodate a 250-pound person without risking structural damage.

Each boat is constructed with 21-pieces of cardboard that are used to make seven component parts. The seven parts are assembled with eco-friendly contact cement and paper drywall tape. Once assembled the boats are sealed with an eco-friendly water-based waterproof coating.

All of the materials used to build a boat can usually be found at 'do-it-yourself' home improvement stores. There are no special tools required and the boats are quite easy to build. People as young as 15 years old have built the boats, by themselves, to the specifications outlined in this book.

The boats can be equipped with 12-volt electric fishing motors, although they are normally propelled with traditional kayak style paddles. Cardboard boats make economical replacements for expensive inflatable boats, kayaks, and canoes for fishing, camping, exploring, exercise, and whatever else you may want to do on the water.

Best-practices safety procedures and the use of Coast Guard approved personal-flotation-devices (PFDs) are considered mandatory to ensure a boater's safety on the water in any watercraft. There isn't anything half as much fun as just messing around in a boat on a sunny day. *The Cardboard Boat Book* shows you how to build a boat for the price of the paint, glue and tape that is required to put one together.

The Cardboard Boat Book

What is Cardboard?

Cardboard is a generic term for a heavy duty paper based product. It is formed with sheets of unbleached craft paper that are pleated and bonded with wood pulp and adhesives to form a strong structure.

Cardboard has inside and outside layers of flat sheets that can resist puncture up to a certain point. The central layer is made from fluted, short fiber paper that not only provides cushioning, but can also resist a certain amount of crushing force.

Cardboard is fully environmentally-friendly as it is made from natural substances, is recyclable and biodegradable, and does not harm the environment.

Three fundamental engineering requirements must be met in order to design a boat. The design must be,

1) Buoyant and stable.
2) Waterproof, or water resistant.
3) Able to support the load requirements.

The cardboard boat designs in this book meet all three engineering requirements.

The buoyancy and stability of the boats in *The Cardboard Boat Book* have been validated by applying the theoretical principles of fluid mechanics to the design of the boats and by many hours of practical testing.

Making the boats structurally strong enough to reliably carry a person, and protecting the boats from water damage, were two major engineering design challenges that had to be solved for the boats to be successfully constructed with cardboard.

To solve the strength requirement, triangular geometric shapes are used throughout the design. Triangles are an inherently stable shape and are one of the strongest shapes of all the basic shapes in the universe. This is why triangular shapes are used in the structural design of many large man-made structures, such as bridges.

As you build the boats in this book you will begin to understand how the triangular shapes of the component parts work together to provide the strength necessary to support the weight of a person.

The triangular shapes are integrated together in a very simple yet elegant design. The design creates an inner framework which provides the structural strength, and at the same time defines an outer surface that determines the volume and shape required to make the boats buoyant and stable. The design is quite clever when you learn how it works. This design methodology can be applied to numerous Hull shapes and corresponding Bow and Stern options.

To solve the challenge of protecting cardboard from water damage a number of waterproof coatings available for protecting wood products were tested. In particular, coatings formulated for waterproofing outdoor wooden structures were researched.

After testing a number of waterproof coatings, products meeting the requirements for being environmentally-friendly were selected as the most desirable for this application.

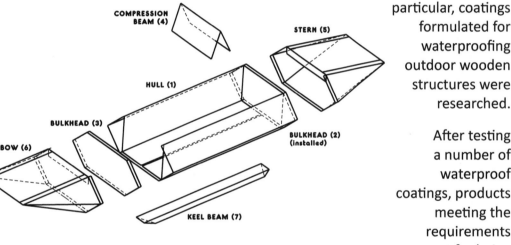

COMPRESSION BEAM (4)
STERN (5)
HULL (1)
BULKHEAD (3)
BOW (6)
BULKHEAD (2) (installed)
KEEL BEAM (7)

To answer the original question, how does a cardboard boat work? A cardboard boat works the same way any boat works. There are unique engineering challenges that required creative solutions and the boat designs presented to you in *The Cardboard Boat Book* incorporate those solutions so that anyone can easily and successfully build their own cardboard boat.

How to Get Started

Step	Five steps to getting started...	Page
1	Choose the Kayaker Design you want to build below	
2	Get the 'Corrugated-Cardboard to Build a Boat'	6&7
3	Get the 'Tools and Materials to Build a Boat'	8
4	Read 'How to Work with Cardboard'	9
5	Read 'Building the Kayaker' and build your boat	10

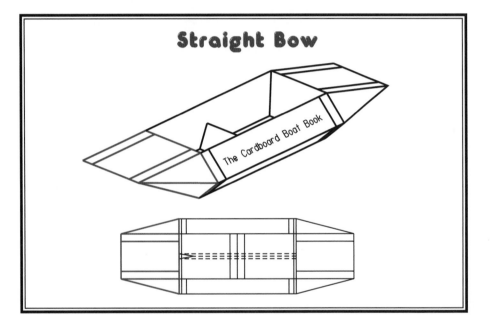

Straight Bow

The Cardboard Boat Book

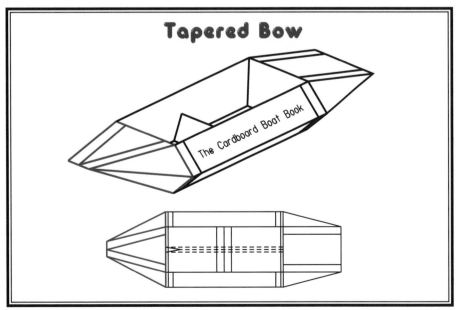

Tapered Bow

The Cardboard Boat Book

Cardboard to Build the Hull

The cardboard pieces needed to build the Hull, and the specific requirements for the Hull cardboard are listed on this page. The cardboard can be new sheets, or recycled boxes in good condition. New sheets are recommended to produce the best looking results.

The cardboard shown on this page will construct 5 of the 7 component parts of a cardboard boat.

Cardboard Requirements for the Hull

1/4-inch thick, 275-lb test, double-wall, corrugated cardboard is required to obtain the necessary strength of the parts.

The corrugation tubes, or flute lines, must run in the direction shown on the sheets below. Read page 9 to learn about corrugation.

You will need the 3-cardboard sheets shown, or equivalent size pieces.

The main body of the Hull requires 1-sheet, 48" x 96". See **Appendix 1** for a 2-piece cardboard Hull construction option.

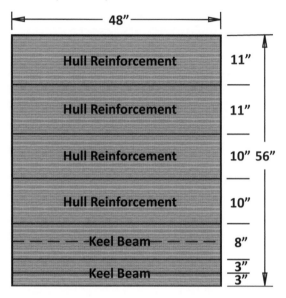

1/4-inch thick, 275-lb test, double-wall corrugated cardboard looks like this

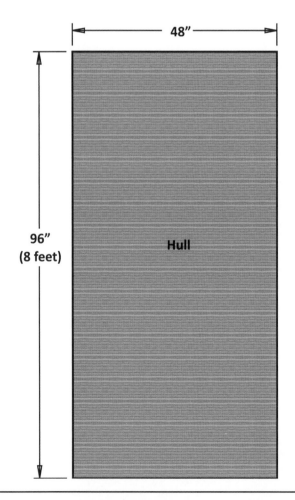

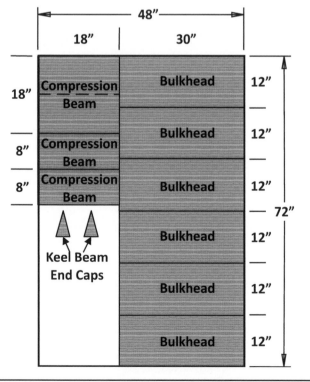

Cardboard to Build the Bow & Stern

The cardboard pieces needed to build the Bow and the Stern, and the specific requirements for the Bow and Stern cardboard are listed on this page.

The cardboard can either be new sheets, or recycled boxes in good condition. New sheets are recommended to produce the best looking results.

The cardboard shown on this page constructs 2 of the 7 component parts of a cardboard boat.

Cardboard Requirements for the Bow and Stern
1/4-inch thick, 275-lb test, double-wall, corrugated cardboard is required to achieve the necessary strength and structural integrity of the parts.
The corrugation tubes, or flute lines, must run in the direction shown on the sheets below. Read page 9 to learn about corrugation.
Construction of the Bow and Stern requires a 60" x 60" sheet of cardboard. If you are unable to locate 60" x 60" sheets you can build the Bow and Stern with the optional 2-piece construction method shown below.
Select either the First or Second option below based on which cardboard you have available.

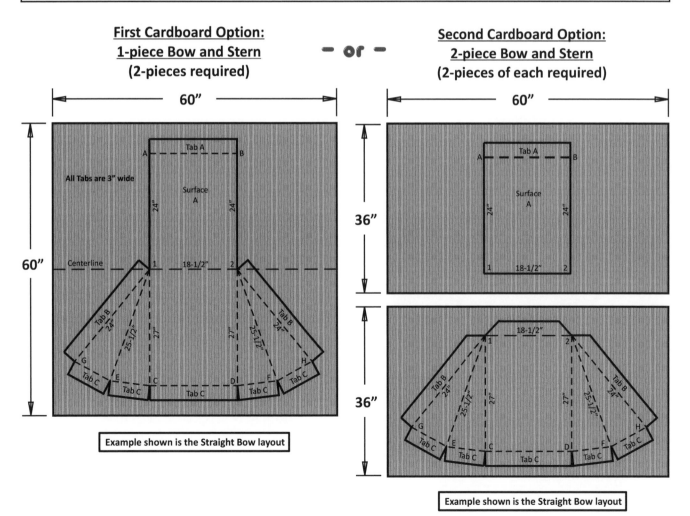

First Cardboard Option:
1-piece Bow and Stern
(2-pieces required)

– or –

Second Cardboard Option:
2-piece Bow and Stern
(2-pieces of each required)

Example shown is the Straight Bow layout

Example shown is the Straight Bow layout

Tools and Materials to Build a Boat

To build a cardboard boat you will need the tools and materials described on this page. The tools and materials are used to:

- Measure and cut pieces of cardboard,
- Construct the component parts of a boat,
- Assemble parts, and
- Finish the boat.

This is the complete list of tools and materials required to construct a cardboard boat. These items can be found at your local home improvement store, or you can search on the Internet to locate them.

	Materials	Used for...
1	1-roll of Paper Drywall Tape (non-sticky type)	taping seams between component parts
2	1/2-gallon of Eco-Friendly Contact Cement	cementing pieces together, assembly, and taping
3	1-gallon of Eco-Friendly Waterproof Coating	waterproofing the cardboard
	Tools	Used for...
4	Pencil	drawing on cardboard
5	8-foot long Tape Measure or longer	measuring lines
6	48-inch long Straightedge	drawing straight lines & folding cardboard
7	Utility Razor Knife	cutting cardboard
8	Screen-Door Spline-Roller (One of many tools that can be used to crease cardboard)	creasing cardboard
9	Simple Beam Compass	drawing Bow and Stern
10	Three 1" & three 2" wide brushes	applying contact cement (inexpensive bristle)
11	One 3" wide inexpensive bristle brush	applying waterproofing coating

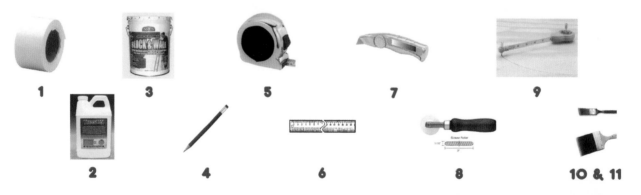

Optional Dent-Resistance Material

The Dent-Resistance material is an optional material that is used to protect your boat from damage under normal operating conditions. You will be given the option of installing the Dent-Resistance material at the end of the construction process. You do not need the Dent-Resistance material to build a cardboard boat.

Read 'Installing Dent-Resistance Material' on page 44 to decide if you want to install this option.

How to Work with Cardboard

The information contained on this page is intended to provide you with 'best practices' procedures for working with cardboard in order to assist you to achieve the best success with your boat building experience.

There are 4 procedures for working with cardboard that you will use throughout the contruction of your boat that you need to be proficient with. The 4 procedures are,

- **Measuring Cardboard**
- **Cutting Cardboard**
- **Creasing and Folding Cardboard**
- **Gluing or Cementing Cardboard**

There is also one important detail regarding the cardboard itself that you need to pay attention to, and be consistent with, when measuring and forming each cardboard part.

-A-

Cardboard is composed of an inner layer, or layers, of fluted corrugation that is sandwiched between layers of paper-board. The flutes form visible lines on the top and bottom surface of a piece of cardboard. (See the flutes in illustration -A- and the visible lines that are formed on the top surface).

The corrugation flutes, or the visible flute lines, must be oriented in a specific direction on each piece of cardboard in order to obtain the strength of the cardboard required to ensure the maximum structural integrity of the finished boat.

The direction the corrugation flute lines need to be oriented are shown in the cardboard pattern on the drawings of each piece of cardboard on the '**Cardboard Required to Build the Hull**' page, and the '**Cardboard Required to Build the Bow and Stern**' page.

Measuring Cardboard

Dimensions are specified in inches and fractions of inches. (Ex: 8-1/4" = 8 and 1/4 inch, or 8.25")

Be exact as possible when measuring and marking dimensions.

A beam compass is highly recommended to accurately draw the shape of the Bow and Stern. (Search the Internet for information on how to make or purchase a simple 'beam compass')

Cutting Cardboard

Place a piece of scrap cardboard under the piece of cardboard you are cutting to protect from damaging the surface below.

Use a utility knife to cut the cardboard and a straightedge to guide your cut in a straight line.

To achieve the cleanest and most accurate cut through a piece of cardboard make two or three passes on each cut. Do not attempt to cut completely through a piece of cardboard in one pass.

Creasing and Folding Cardboard

Align a straightedge along the line you want to crease. Hold the spline-roller against the straightedge. Press down firmly on the spline-roller, and roll along the entire length of the crease line, crushing the cardboard corrugation to weaken it.

Keeping the straightedge in place, gently lift up on the cardboard to initiate a fold in the cardboard.

Gluing or Cementing Cardboard

Apply contact cement to both mating surfaces of cardboard. Allow contact cement to dry according to manufacturers recommendations before contacting the pieces of cardboard together.

Carefully align the two cemented surfaces before making contact between them. Then press the surfaces together.

Direction of Corrugation Flute Lines

Read and follow the requirements on this page.

Building The Kayaker

Specification:

8-feet long

~

1-foot deep

~

2-1/2 feet wide

~

Weighs approx. 25 pounds

~

Accommodates up to a
250 lb person

COMPRESSION BEAM (4)

HULL (1)

BULKHEAD (3)

BOW (6)

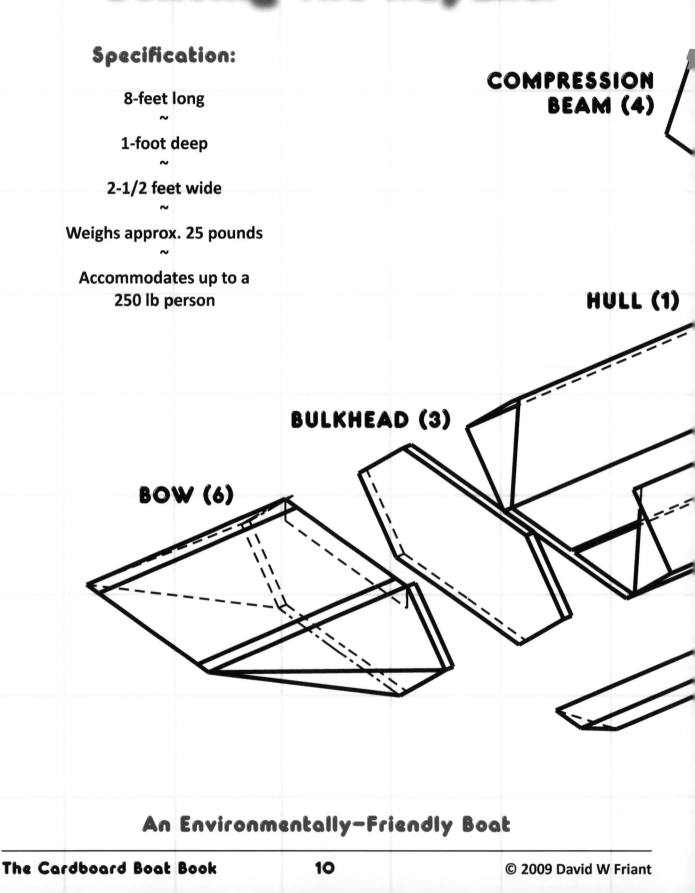

An Environmentally-Friendly Boat

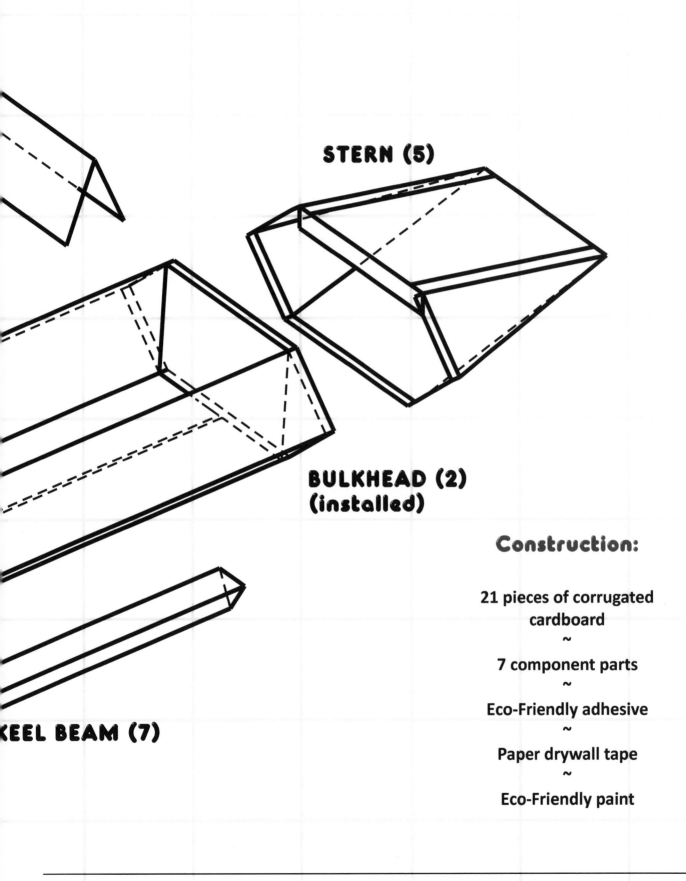

STERN (5)

**BULKHEAD (2)
(installed)**

KEEL BEAM (7)

Construction:

21 pieces of corrugated
cardboard
~
7 component parts
~
Eco-Friendly adhesive
~
Paper drywall tape
~
Eco-Friendly paint

The Kayaker is constructed with 21 pieces of cardboard of different shapes and sizes. The individual pieces are shown on pages 6 and 7.

Seven (7) component parts are made with the 21 pieces of cardboard. The instruction process walks you through building the seven component parts in the order they are assembled.

All tools and materials required to build a boat are itemized and pictured on page 8.

The seven components are shown in the 'Unassembled View' of the Kayaker on pages 10 and 11 and are listed below.
1) Hull
2) Bulkhead 1
3) Bulkhead 2
4) Compression Beam
5) Stern
6) Bow (select from 2 Bow designs shown on page 5 and 28)
7) Keel Beam

An explanation of how to work with cardboard including, measuring cardboard, cutting cardboard, creasing and folding cardboard, and cementing cardboard together is discussed on page 9.

The building instructions are explained in the order that a boat is constructed. A 3-step instruction process describes the construction of each of the 7 component parts and the boat is assembled as the components are completed. The three step process includes,
1) Written instructions with a detailed drawing of each individual piece of cardboard required for the part.
2) A 3-dimensional assembly diagram of the part.
3) A photo or series of photos of the finished part and photos of the completed assembly.

After the boat is fully assembled, the seams between component parts and exposed edges of cardboard are sealed with paper drywall tape using contact cement to adhere the tape to the cardboard. DO NOT use sticky-back drywall tape. The tape MUST be adhered to the cardboard with contact cement to ensure the required seal is achieved in preparation for waterproofing your boat.

You will be given the choice of installing optional Dent-Resistant material to designated edges of the boats exterior prior to taping the boat. The Dent-Resistant material is NOT REQUIRED to build a boat. The sole purpose of the Dent-Resistant material is to keep your boat looking good as long as possible and protects vulnerable edges of the cardboard from being damaged during normal use.

Once your boat is taped it is ready to be waterproofed and personalized. I recommend that you read through each set of instructions before performing the steps that are described.

I also highly recommend that when you get to the steps that require cementing cardboard together with contact cement, you practice performing the task before actually applying the contact cement in order to ensure you completely understand how to perform the task and have a plan for completing the task.

This is recommended because when two parts that have contact cement on them make contact with each other you WILL NOT be able to move or separate the parts from each other without destroying the cardboard.

If you have not done so already please read the page titled **How to Get Started** before you begin construction of the Kayaker. That page outlines what you need to do before you start to build.

The detailed instructions to build your Kayaker start on the next page beginning with the Hull construction.

Hull Construction

Step 1: Lay the 48" x 96" sheet of cardboard out flat on the floor. (If you do not have a standard 48" x 96" sheet of cardboard see Appendix 1 for a Hull Construction option using two pieces of cardboard). The corrugation flutes run the 48" width of the sheet.

Use the tape measure to locate and mark the middle of the sheet with the pencil and draw a line through the center of the sheet to be used as a reference line. See **figure 1**. (DO NOT CREASE THIS LINE.)

Step 2: Working from the centerline of the sheet, measure and draw the 8 crease-lines as shown towards both ends of the sheet. Number the crease-lines as you draw them as shown on **figure 2**.

When you are done there should be 8 crease lines and one centerline drawn on the sheet.

Trim the excess few inches off of both ends of the cardboard sheet after you have measured and drawn all of the crease-lines.

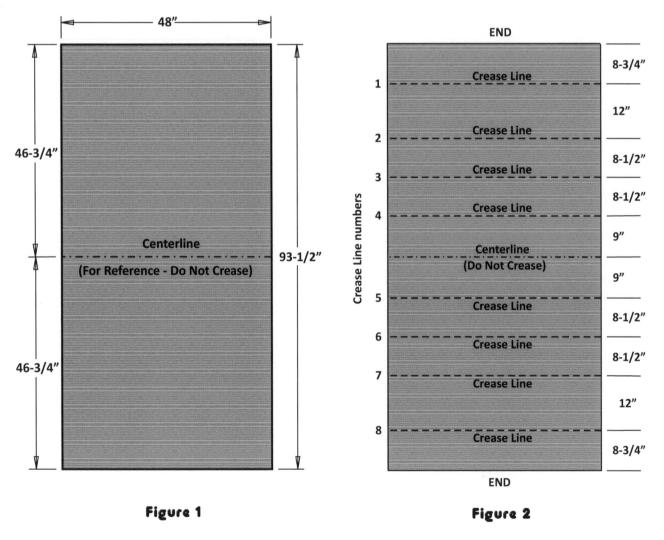

Figure 1

Locate the centerline of the Hull

Figure 2

Measure and draw the crease lines

The areas between the 8 crease-lines are referred to as panels. There are 9 panels on the sheet. The center panel, #5, has two halves, labeled 5a and 5b, on either side of the centerline. Number the 9 panels as shown on **figure 3**.

Step 3: Cut a 1"-wide by 2-panel long strip of cardboard from each corner of the Hull sheet as shown in **figure 4**. (This cutout will accommodate the Bulkhead installation).

Step 4: Measure and cut the 4 Hull reinforcement panels to shape as shown on page 6 and in **figure 5**. (2 panels measure 10" x 46" and 2 panels measure 11" x 46").

Step 5: Cement the 11" wide reinforcement panels to the center of Hull panels 2 and 8 as shown in **figures 5, 6 and 7**.

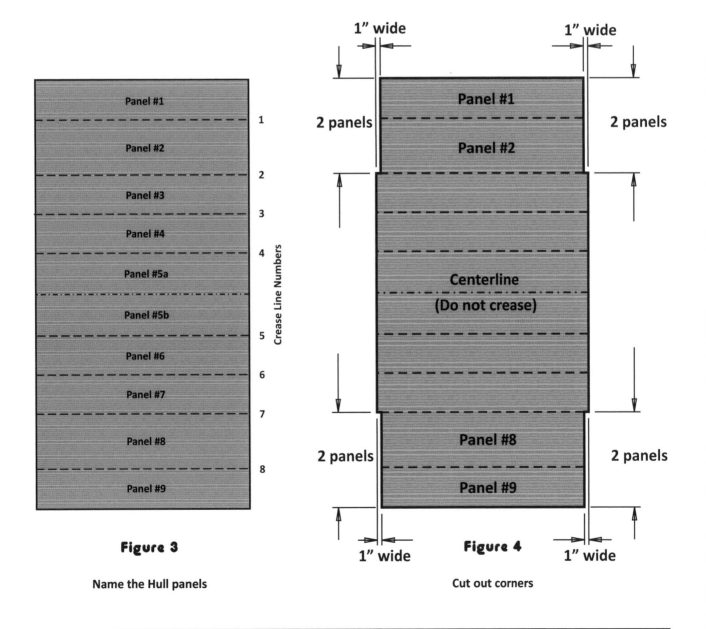

Figure 3

Name the Hull panels

Figure 4

Cut out corners

Step 6: Cement the 10" wide reinforcement panels to the center of the 11" wide panels as shown in **figure 5, 6 and 7**.

Crease the 8 crease-lines in preparation for folding the Hull into shape. (**Note:** Panels 1 & 9 fold away from the sheet therefore crease-lines 1 and 8 need to be creased on the opposite side of the sheet.)

Step7: Fold the Hull sheet into its shape. Cement panel 1 to panel 5a. Cement panel 9 to panel 5b. See **figures 7, 8, 9, & 10** in succession. Also see **photos 1, 2, & 3,** to visualize the process of folding the Hull into shape.

The outside edge of panel 1 and panel 9 should meet at the center of the Hull. If they overlap each other, trim the panels to the correct width. If they don't meet at the centerline, cut a piece of cardboard to fill in the gap between the two panels.

When properly cemented together your Hull should look like **figure 10** and **photo 3**.

DONE Proceed to **Bulkhead Construction.**

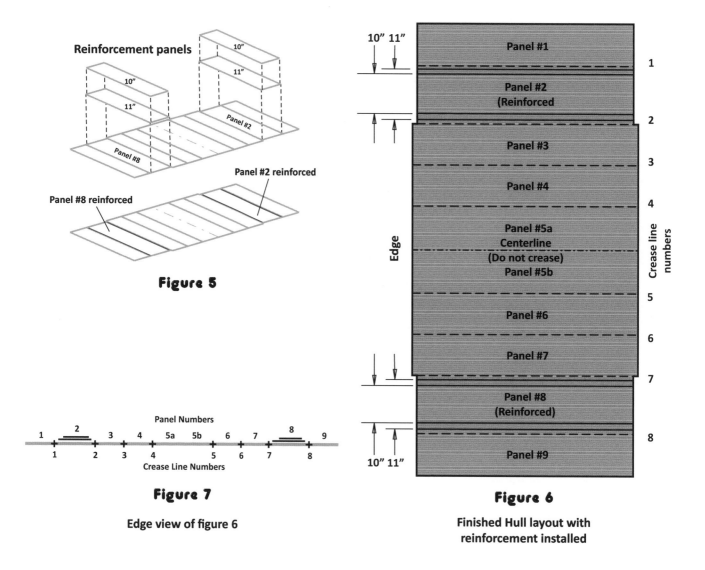

Figure 5

Figure 7

Edge view of figure 6

Figure 6

Finished Hull layout with reinforcement installed

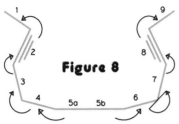

Figure 8

Edge view of the Hull
as it is being folded into shape

Photo 1

First side folded in place

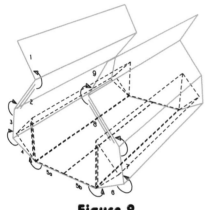

Figure 9

3D view of folding the Hull

Photo 2

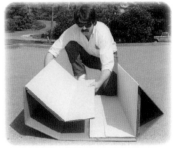

Second side being folded

The outside edge of panels 1 and 9
meet at the centerline

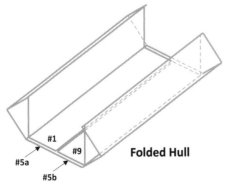

Folded Hull

Figure 10

Photo 3

Folded Hull

Step 1: Measure, draw, and cut out the six 12" x 30" pieces of cardboard, shown on page 6, to construct the Bulkheads. Be sure the corrugation flutes run the 30" width of each of the 6 pieces.

Measure 6" in from the corner of each 12" x 30" rectangle piece of cardboard. Cut off the marked pieces as shown. The result is the 4 sides are 8-1/4" each, and the top and bottom are 18". Make slight adjustments if required to achieve these dimensions. See **figures 1 & 2.**

Step 2: Construct one Bulkhead by cementing 3 pieces of cardboard together. See **figure 3**.

Step 3: Construct the second Bulkhead by cementing 3 pieces of cardboard together. See **figure 3**.

Step 4: Cement the bulkheads into the cutout in both ends of the Hull at the same time. This procedure is best accomplished with two people working together. One person guides one Bulkhead into position while the other person guides the second Bulkhead into position. **Figure 4** shows where to apply the cement.

Step 5: First, cement the bottom of the Bulkheads into position. Second, have both people lift up one side of the Hull and press the Hull onto the Bulkheads. Third, have both people lift the other side of the Hull up and press the Hull onto the Bulkheads. Ensure you have a consistent bond between the Bulkheads and the cutout in the Hull. Refer to **Photos 2,3,&4.** to visualize the procedure.

When the Bulkheads are installed your boat should look like **photo 5 and figure 5**.

NOTE: Fitting the Bulkhead into the ends of the Hull requires patience. Practice the procedure before applying the contact cement to ensure you get the Bulkheads installed successfully.

DONE Proceed to **Compression Beam Construction.**

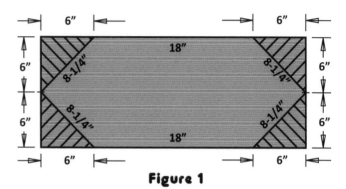

Figure 1

Measuring the dimensions of the pieces

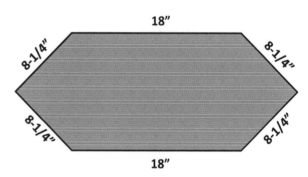

Figure 2

Finished pieces with correct dimensions

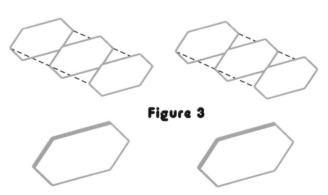

Figure 3

Constructing the 2 Bulkheads with 3-pieces each

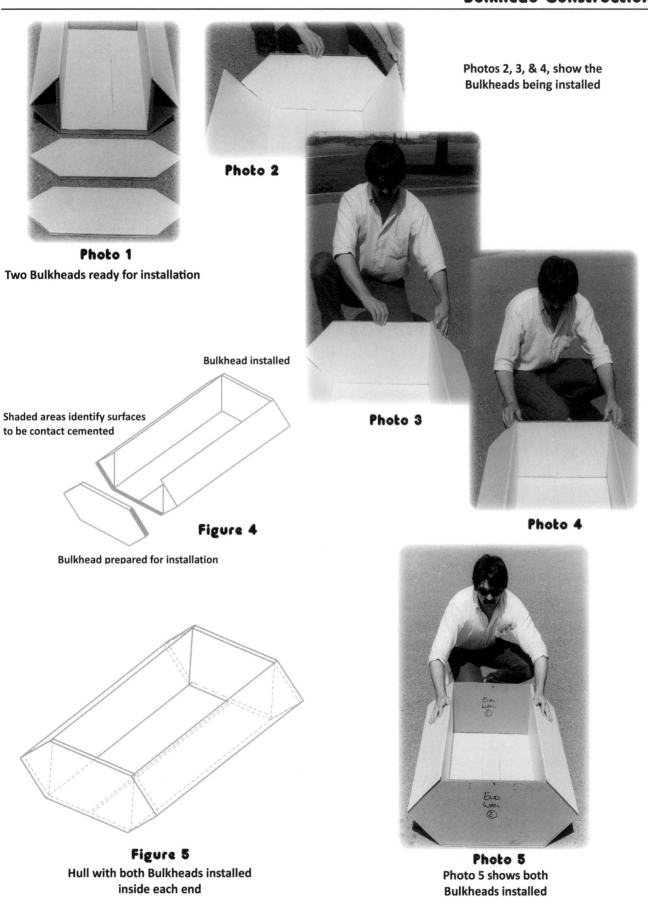

Photo 1
Two Bulkheads ready for installation

Photos 2, 3, & 4, show the Bulkheads being installed

Photo 2

Photo 3

Photo 4

Bulkhead installed

Shaded areas identify surfaces to be contact cemented

Figure 4

Bulkhead prepared for installation

Figure 5
Hull with both Bulkheads installed inside each end

Photo 5
Photo 5 shows both Bulkheads installed

Compression Beam Construction

Step 1: Measure, draw, and cut out the 3 pieces of cardboard to construct the Compression Beam as shown on page 6 and in **figure 1**. Be sure the corrugation flutes run the 18" width of each piece.

CONSTRUCTION NOTE: If the boat will be limited to carrying a person and supplies weighing less than a total of 125-pounds, the height of the Compression Beam can be reduced to a height of 6-inches. The standard Compression Beam height is 9-inches.

Step 2: Cement the reinforcement pieces to the Compression Beam as shown in **figure 2 and 3**.

Step 3: Crease and fold the Compression Beam in half with the reinforcement pieces on the inside and the sides of the beam 6-inches apart as shown in **figures 4 & 5**.

While holding the Compression Beam 6" apart rub the bottom edges of the Beam back and forth against a concrete or asphalt floor to shape the edges of the Beam flat against the ground. This will ensure a good bond is achieved between the bottom of the Beam and the floor of the Hull.

Step 4: Locate the Compression Beam in the center of the Hull and mark its location with a pencil as shown in **figure 6**. Then cement the Compression Beam to the inside of the Hull.

When the compression Beam is installed your boat will look like **photo 1 and figure 6**.

DONE Proceed to the **Stern Construction.**

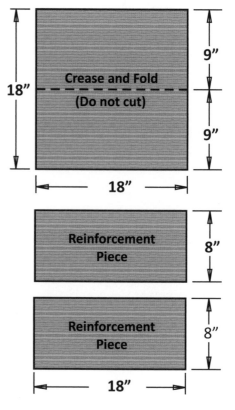

Figure 1
Three Compression Beam pieces with dimensions

What is the purpose of the Compression Beam?

The purpose of the Compression Beam is to maintain the shape of the Hull by keeping the sides of the Hull walls from buckling inwards due to the force of a person sitting in the boat. The Compression Beam is under a compression force and this is why it is called the Compression Beam. See the Construction Note in step 1 for information on a Compression Beam design option.

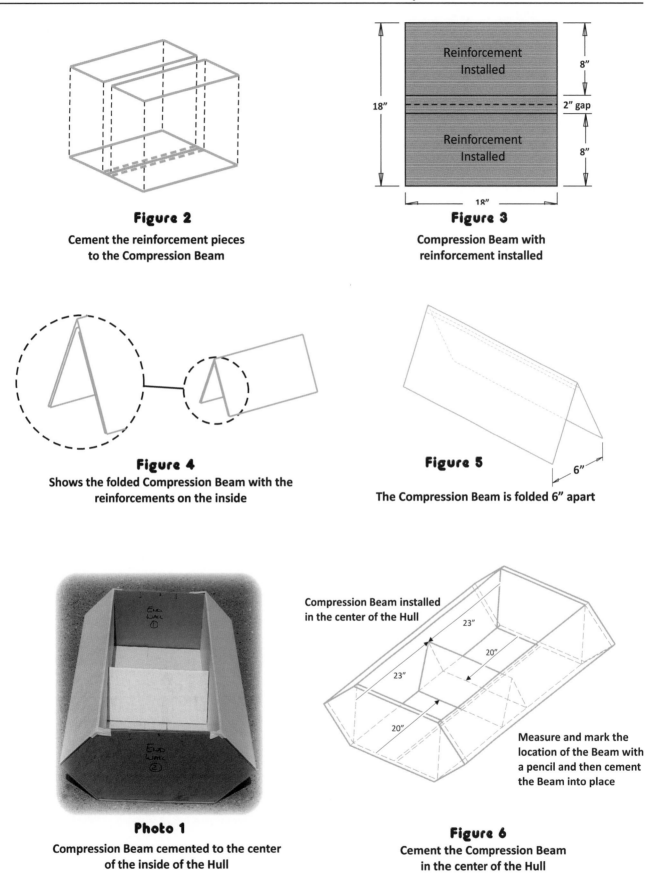

Figure 2

Cement the reinforcement pieces
to the Compression Beam

Figure 3

Compression Beam with
reinforcement installed

Figure 4

Shows the folded Compression Beam with the
reinforcements on the inside

Figure 5

The Compression Beam is folded 6" apart

Photo 1

Compression Beam cemented to the center
of the inside of the Hull

Compression Beam installed
in the center of the Hull

Measure and mark the
location of the Beam with
a pencil and then cement
the Beam into place

Figure 6

Cement the Compression Beam
in the center of the Hull

Stern Construction

Step 1: Lay the Stern cardboard sheet out flat on the floor. Pay attention to the direction of the corrugation flutes. Be sure the corrugation flutes run perpendicular to the centerline as shown.

Draw a line through the center of the sheet and mark this line as the centerline as shown in **figure 1.**

Locate and mark the center of the sheet as shown in **figure 1**.

Step 2: Locate point 1, 9-1/4" along the centerline from the center of the sheet. Locate point 2, 9-1/4" along the centerline from the center of the sheet. Points 1 & 2 should be 18-1/2" apart from each other. See **figure 2.**

Step 3: Measure straight up 25" perpendicular from points 1 & 2 to locate points A & B. Measure straight down 25" perpendicular from points 1 & 2 to locate points C & D as shown in **figure 2.**

The distance between points A & B, 1 & 2, and C & D, must be 18-1/2" each.

Step 4: Connect points A to B, 1 to 2, and C to D. Connect points A to C, and B to D, with a line using the pencil and the straightedge.

Step 5: Get out your beam compass to draw the angled lines for the Stern. Refer to **figure 3** for steps 5 through 10.

Set your compass length at 8-1/2". Place the pivot point of your compass at point C and strike an arc towards the left of point C. Place the pivot point of your compass at point D and strike an arc towards the right of point D as shown.

Step 6: Set your compass to 25". Place the pivot point of your compass at point 1 and mark point E at the intersection with the 8-1/2" arc. Ensure the length of the line between point 1 and point E is 25".

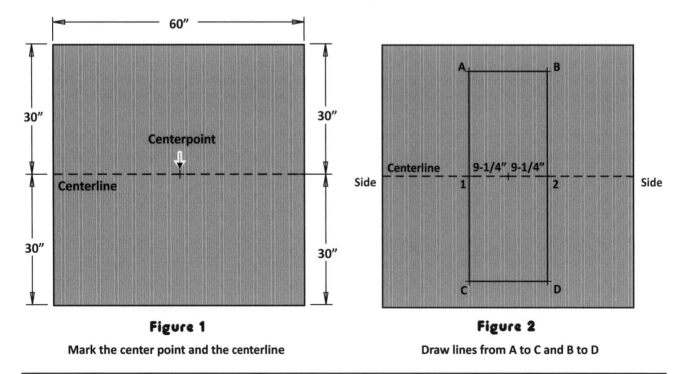

Figure 1

Mark the center point and the centerline

Figure 2

Draw lines from A to C and B to D

Step 7: Set your compass to 25". Place the pivot point of your compass at point 2 and mark point F at the intersection with the 8-1/2" arc. Ensure the length of the line between point 2 and point F is 25".

Step 8: Set your compass length at 8-1/2". Place the pivot point of your compass at point E and strike an arc towards the left of point E. Place the pivot point of your compass at point F and strike an arc towards the right of point F.

Step 9: Set your compass to 25". Place the pivot point of your compass at point 1 and mark point G at the intersection with the 8-1/2" arc. Ensure the length of the line between point 1 and point G is 25".

Step 10: Set your compass to 25". Place the pivot point of your compass at point 2 and mark point H at the intersection with the 8-1/2" arc. Ensure the length of the line between point 2 and point H is 25".

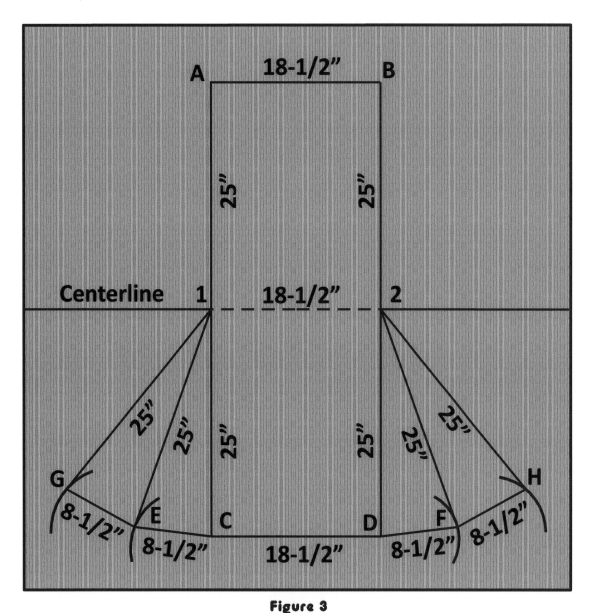

Figure 3
Draw the angled lines as explained
in steps 5 through 10.

 The Cardboard Boat Book

Step 11: Using a pencil and straightedge connect the points together with lines. When you have completed the steps above your Stern drawing should look like **figure 3**.

Step 12: Draw 3"-wide tabs as shown around the sides of the drawing of the Stern as shown on **figure 4**. Tabs are labeled Tab A, Tab B, and Tabs C. Label the tabs as shown in **figure 4**.

Step 14: Cut the drawing of the Stern out of the sheet of cardboard as shown in **figure 5**.

Step 14: Crease and fold all dashed lines shown in **figure 4.**

Step 15: Fold and cement the Stern together to create its shape as shown in **figures 6 and 7** and explained in **Step 16, photos 1 through 5,** on page 26.

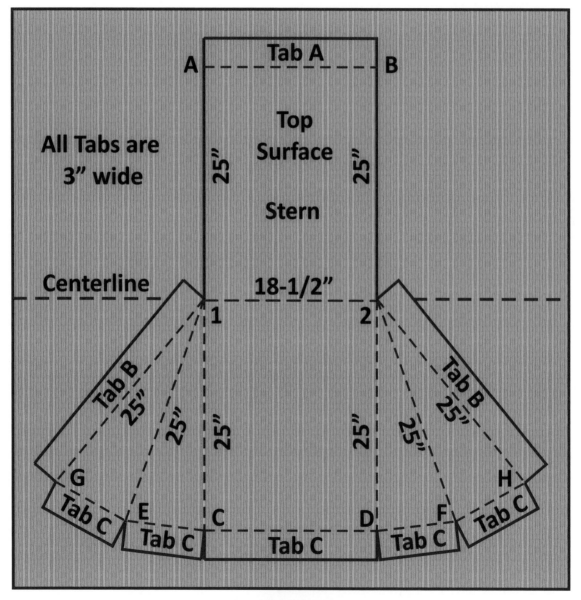

Figure 4

Draw and label the Tabs

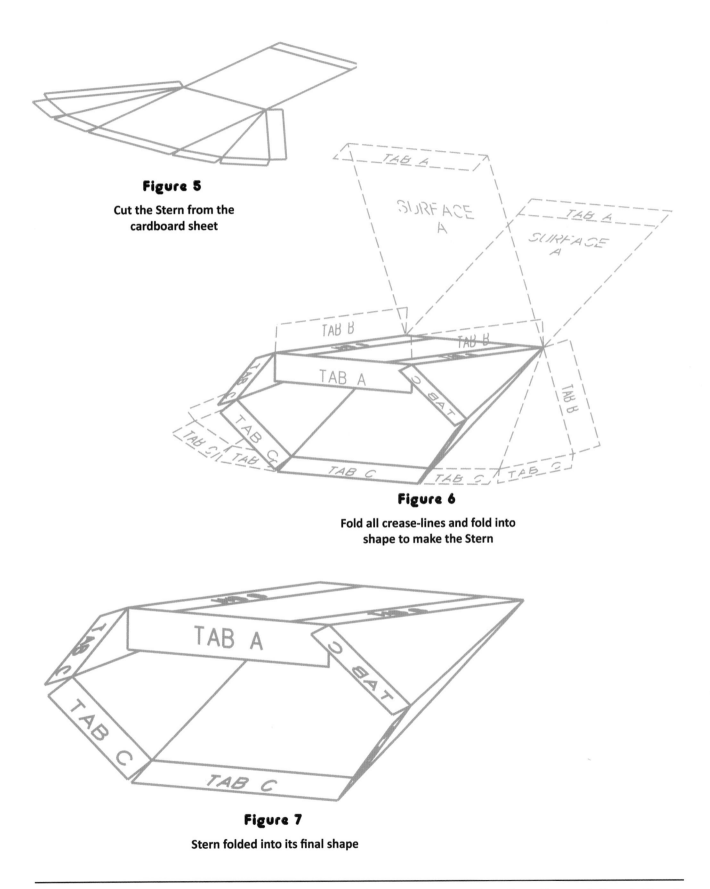

Figure 5

Cut the Stern from the
cardboard sheet

SURFACE
A

TAB A

SURFACE
A

TAB A

TAB B

TAB B

TAB A

TAB B

TAB C

TAB C

TAB C

TAB C

TAB C

Figure 6

Fold all crease-lines and fold into
shape to make the Stern

TAB A

TAB C

TAB C

Figure 7

Stern folded into its final shape

The Cardboard Boat Book

Step 16: Review **photos 1 through 5** to learn how the Stern is folded into shape.

When you are ready to cement the Stern together, apply contact cement to the inside of 'Tabs B' and to the Top Surface where 'Tabs B' will make contact. Then cement Tabs B to the Top Surface as shown as shown in **photos 3, 4, & 5.**

DONE When you finish building the Stern, as shown in **photo 5**, proceed to page 35 for instructions on how to install the Stern to the Hull, or, proceed to the **Bow Design Options** on page 28 if you want to construct the Bow before installing both the Stern and Bow.

Photo 3

Applying contact cement to Tabs B

Photo 4

Cementing Tabs B to the Top Surface

Photo 1

Folding the crease-lines

Photo 2

Folding the Stern to shape

Photo 5

Stern cemented together and ready for installation

Bow Design Options

There are two design options for the Bow. There is a 'Straight Bow' design and a 'Tapered Bow' design. Choose one of the two Bow designs, shown below and at the right, for your boat.

Bow 1: Straight Bow Construction and Installation	
NOTE	The Straight Bow is constructed and installed in the same manner as the Stern is constructed and installed. The difference is that the dimensions of the Straight Bow are different than the Stern and it is positioned flush with the top edge of the boat.
	Proceed to constructing the Straight Bow on page 30.

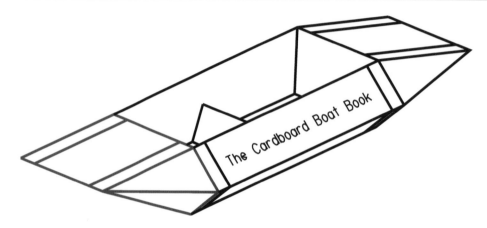

Bow 2: Tapered Bow Construction and Installation	
NOTE	The Tapered Bow is constructed and installed in the same manner as the Stern is constructed and installed. The difference is that the dimensions and shape of the Tapered Bow are different than the Stern and Straight Bow.
	Proceed to constructing the Tapered Bow on page 36.

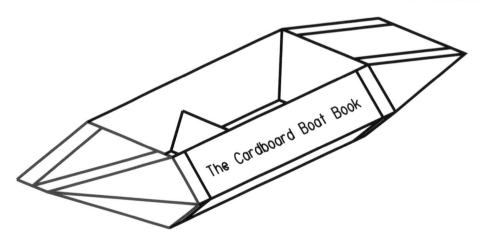

Straight Bow Dimensions

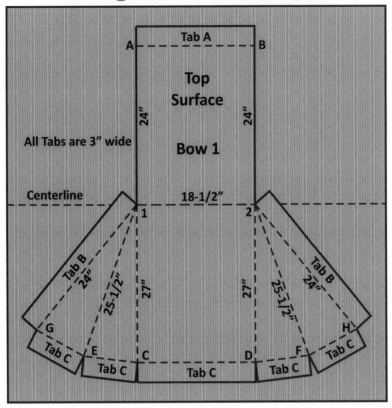

Tapered Bow Dimensions

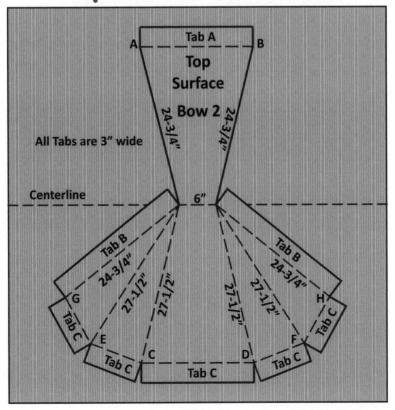

Bow 1: Straight Bow Construction

Step 1: Lay the Bow cardboard sheet out flat on the floor. Pay attention to the direction of the corrugation flutes. Be sure the corrugation flutes run perpendicular to the centerline as shown.

Draw a line through the center of the sheet and mark this line as the centerline as shown in **figure 1.**

Locate and mark the center of the sheet as shown in **figure 1**.

Step 2: Locate point 1, 9-1/4" along the centerline from the center of the sheet. Locate point 2, 9-1/4" along the centerline from the center of the sheet. Points 1 & 2 should be 18-1/2" apart from each other. See **figure 2.**

Step 3: Measure straight up 24" perpendicular from points 1 & 2 to locate points A & B. Measure straight down 27" perpendicular from points 1 & 2 to locate points C & D as shown in **figure 2.**

The distance between points A & B, 1 & 2, and C & D, must be 18-1/2" each.

Step 4: Connect points A to B, 1 to 2, and C to D. Connect points A to C, and B to D, with a line using the pencil and the straightedge.

Step 5: Get out your beam compass to draw the angled lines for the Bow. Refer to **figure 3** for steps 5 through 10.

Set your compass length at 8-1/2". Place the pivot point of your compass at point C and strike an arc towards the left of point C. Place the pivot point of your compass at point D and strike an arc towards the right of point D as shown.

Step 6: Set your compass to 25-1/2". Place the pivot point of your compass at point 1 and mark point E at the intersection with the 8-1/2" arc. Ensure the length of the line between point 1 and point E is 25-1/2".

Figure 1

Mark the center point and the centerline

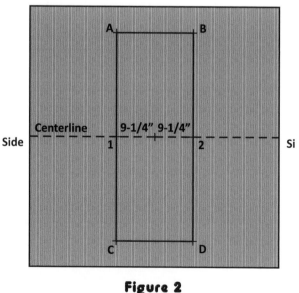

Figure 2

Draw lines from A to C and B to D

Step 7: Set your compass to 25-1/2". Place the pivot point of your compass at point 2 and mark point F at the intersection with the 8-1/2" arc. Ensure the length of the line between point 2 and point F is 25-1/2".

Step 8: Set your compass length at 8-1/2". Place the pivot point of your compass at point E and strike an arc towards the left of point E. Place the pivot point of your compass at point F and strike an arc towards the right of point F.

Step 9: Set your compass to 24". Place the pivot point of your compass at point 1 and mark point G at the intersection with the 8-1/2" arc. Ensure the length of the line between point 1 and point G is 24".

Step 10: Set your compass to 24". Place the pivot point of your compass at point 2 and mark point H at the intersection with the 8-1/2" arc. Ensure the length of the line between point 2 and point H is 24".

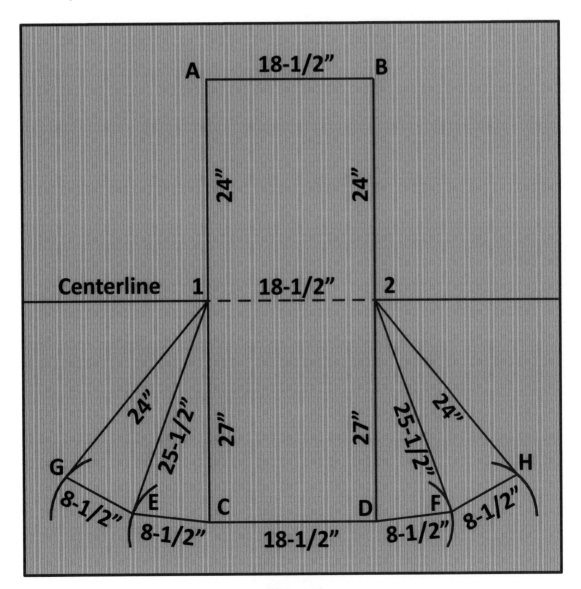

Figure 3
Draw the angled lines as explained
in steps 5 through 10.

Step 11: Using a pencil and straightedge connect the points together with lines. When you have completed the steps above your Bow drawing should look like **figure 3**.

Step 12: Draw 3"-wide tabs as shown around the sides of the drawing of the Bow as shown on **figure 4**. Tabs are labeled Tab A, Tab B, and Tabs C. Label the tabs as shown in **figure 4**.

Step 13: Cut the drawing of the Bow out of the sheet of cardboard as shown in **figure 5**.

Step 14: Crease and fold all dotted lines shown in **figure 4**.

Step 15: Fold and cement the Bow together to create its shape as shown in **figures 6 and 7** and explained in **Step 16, photos 1 through 5,** on page 34.

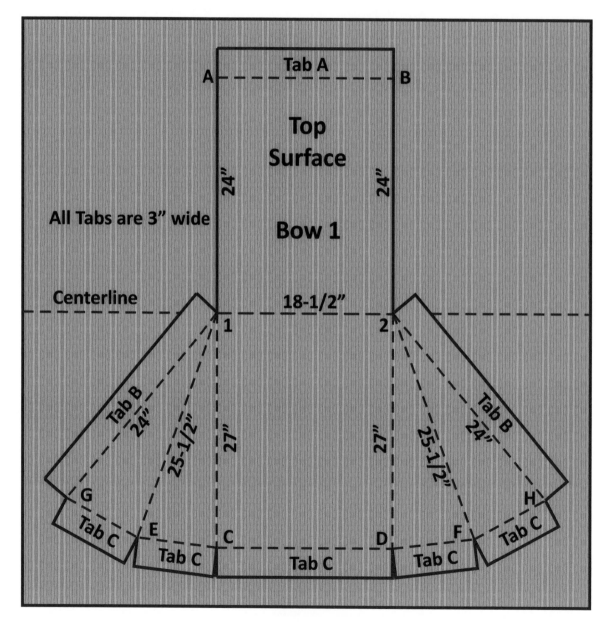

Figure 4

Draw and label the Tabs

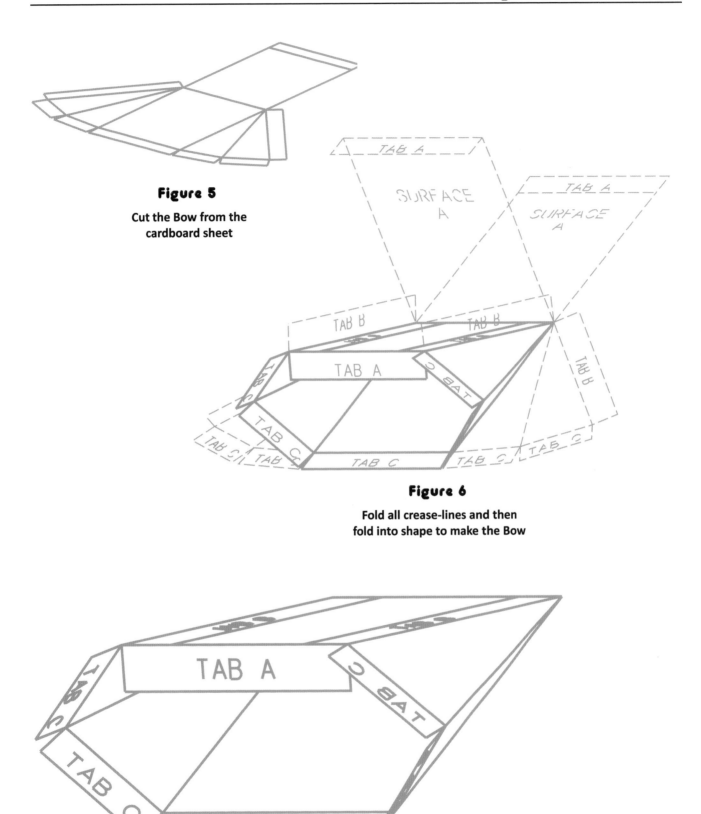

Figure 5

Cut the Bow from the
cardboard sheet

Figure 6

Fold all crease-lines and then
fold into shape to make the Bow

Figure 7

Bow folded into its final shape

Step 16: Review **photos 1 through 5** to learn how the Bow is folded into shape.

When you are ready to cement the Bow together, apply contact cement to the inside of 'Tabs B' and to the Top Surface where 'Tabs B' will make contact. Then cement Tabs B to the Top Surface as shown as shown in **photos 3, 4, & 5.**

DONE When you finish building the Bow, as shown in **photo 5**, proceed to **Installing the Stern and Bow** for instructions on how to attach the Stern and the Bow to the Hull.

Photo 3

Applying contact
cement to Tabs B

Photo 1

Folding the crease-lines

Photo 4

Cementing Tabs B to
the Top Surface

Photo 2

Folding the Stern to shape

Photo 5

Stern cemented together
and ready for installation

Installing the Stern and Bow

Step 1: Align the Stern or the Bow with the Hull to ensure it will install correctly as shown in **photo 6.**

'Tab A' of the Stern or Bow butts up and cements to the end of the Bulkhead as shown in **photo 7 and figure 8.** 'Tabs C' cement to the outside of the end of the Hull as shown in **photo 8 and figure 8.**

Step 2: When you are ready to cement the Stern or Bow to the Hull, apply contact cement to the outside of 'Tab A' and the end of the Bulkhead, and the inside of 'Tabs C' and to a 3"-width around the outside of the end of the Hull as shown in **figure 8.**

Step 3: When the contact cement is dry, align the Stern or Bow onto the end of the Hull. First press 'Tab A' to the outside of the Bulkhead on the end of the Hull. Second, rotate the Stern or Bow back into place and press 'Tabs C' onto the end of the Hull.

DONE When you complete the installation of the Stern and Bow proceed to the **Keel Beam Construction.**

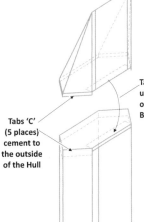

Tab 'A' butts up against the outside of the Bulkhead

Tabs 'C' (5 places) cement to the outside of the Hull

Figure 8

Proper placement of Tabs

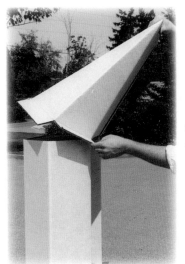

Photo 7

Cement Tab A to the end of the Bulkhead without allowing Tabs C to make contact

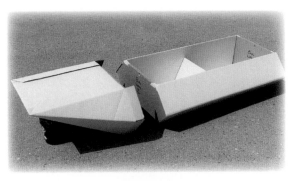

Photo 6

Check for proper alignment

Photo 8

Rotate the Stern, or Bow, downwards to allow Tabs C to make contact with the Hull

Bow 2: Tapered Bow Construction

Step 1: Lay the Bow cardboard sheet out flat on the floor. Pay attention to the direction of the corrugation flutes. Be sure the corrugation flutes run perpendicular to the centerline as shown.

Draw a line through the center of the sheet and mark this line as the centerline as shown in **figure 1.**

Locate and mark the center of the sheet as shown in **figure 1**.

Step 2: Locate point 1, 3" along the centerline from the center of the sheet. Locate point 2, 3" along the centerline from the center of the sheet. Points 1 & 2 should be 6" apart from each other. See **figure 1.**

Step 3: Measure straight up 24" perpendicular from points 1 & 2 to locate points 3 & 4. Measure straight down 26-3/4" perpendicular from points 1 & 2 to locate points 5 & 6 as shown in **figure 1.** Measure 6-1/4" over from points 3, 4, 5 & 6 to locate points A, B, C, & D, as shown in **figure 2.**

The distance between points A & B, and C & D, must both be 18-1/2". The distance between points 1 & 2 must be 6".

Step 4: Connect points A to B, and C to D. Connect points A to 1, 1 to C, B to 2, and 2 to D, with a line using the pencil and straightedge as shown in **figure 2.**

Step 5: Use your beam compass to draw the angled lines for the Bow. Refer to **figure 3** for steps 5 through 10.

Set your compass length at 8-1/2". Place the pivot point of your compass at point C and strike an arc towards the left of point C. Place the pivot point of your compass at point D and strike an arc towards the right of point D as shown.

Step 6: Set your compass to 27-1/2". Place the pivot point of your compass at point 1 and mark point E at the intersection with the 8-1/2" arc. Ensure the length of the line between point 1 and point E is 27-1/2".

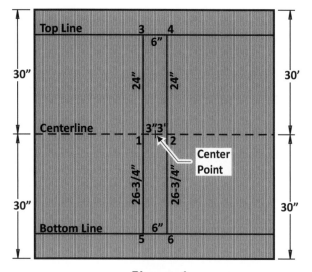

Figure 1

Mark the center point and the centerline

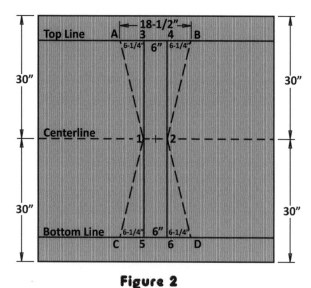
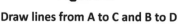

Figure 2

Draw lines from A to C and B to D

Step 7: Set your compass to 27-1/2". Place the pivot point of your compass at point 2 and mark point F at the intersection with the 8-1/2" arc. Ensure the length of the line between point 2 and point F is 27-1/2".

Step 8: Set your compass length at 8-1/2". Place the pivot point of your compass at point E and strike an arc towards the left of point E. Place the pivot point of your compass at point F and strike an arc towards the right of point F.

Step 9: Set your compass to 24-3/4". Place the pivot point of your compass at point 1 and mark point G at the intersection with the 8-1/2" arc. Ensure the length of the line between point 1 and point G is 24-3/4".

Step 10: Set your compass to 24-3/4". Place the pivot point of your compass at point 2 and mark point H at the intersection with the 8-1/2" arc. Ensure the length of the line between point 2 and point H is 24-3/4".

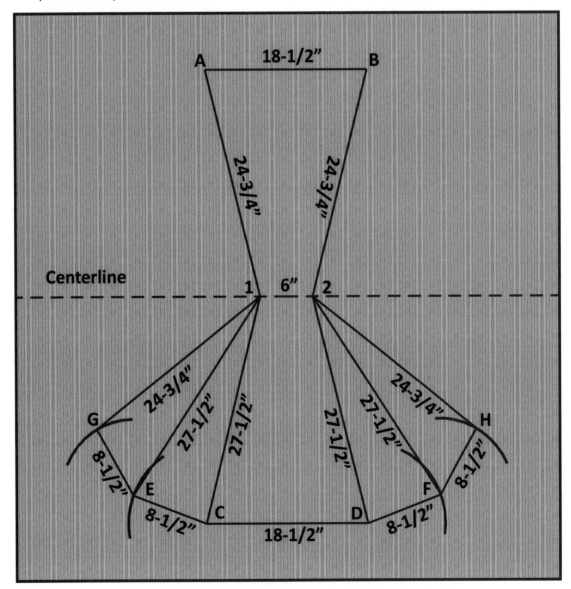

Figure 3
Draw the angled lines as explained
in steps 5 through 10.

Step 11: Using a pencil and straightedge connect the points together with lines. When you have completed the steps above your Bow drawing should look like **figure 3**.

Step 12: Draw 3"-wide tabs as shown around the sides of the drawing of the Bow as shown on **figure 4**. Tabs are labeled Tab A, Tab B, and Tabs C. Label the tabs as shown in **figure 4**.

Step 13: Cut the drawing of the Bow out of the sheet of cardboard as shown in **figure 5**.

Step 14: Crease and fold all dotted lines shown in **figure 4**.

Step 15: Fold and cement the Bow together to create its shape as shown in **figures 6 and 7** and explained on page 34, **Step 16, photos 1 through 5**.

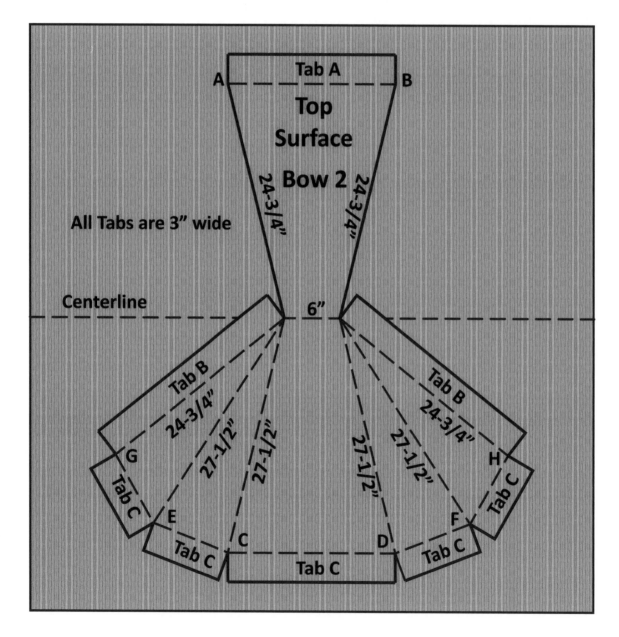

Figure 4

Draw and label the Tabs

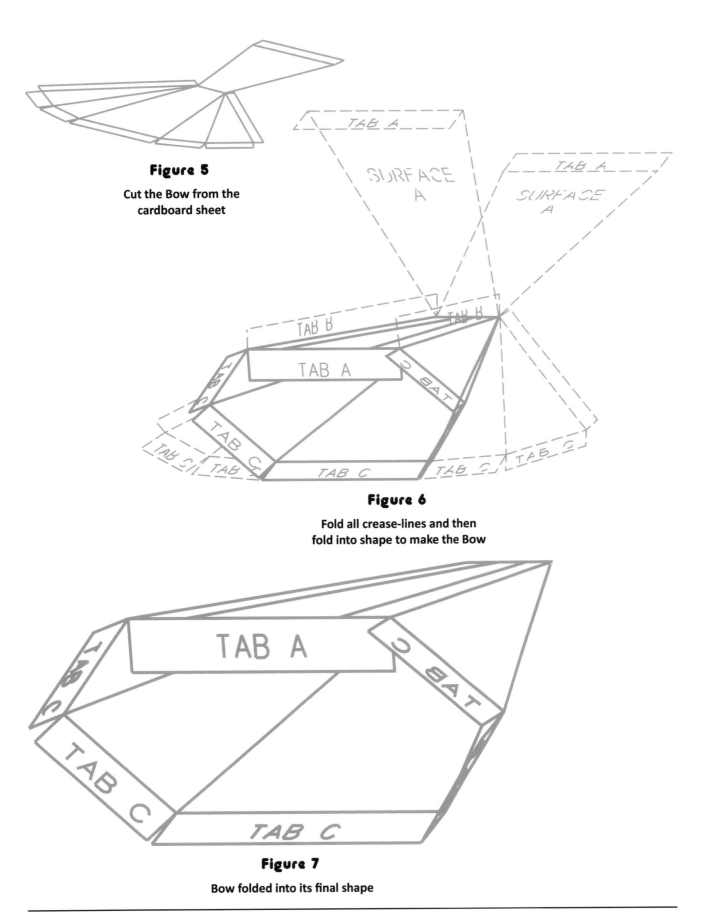

Figure 5

Cut the Bow from the
cardboard sheet

Figure 6

Fold all crease-lines and then
fold into shape to make the Bow

Figure 7

Bow folded into its final shape

Keel Beam Construction

Step 1: Measure, draw, and cut out the 3 pieces of cardboard to construct the Keel Beam as shown in **figure 1 & 2**. Be sure the corrugation flutes run the length of the cardboard as shown.

Step 2: Cement the reinforcement pieces to the Keel Beam as shown in **figure 3 & 5**.

Step 3: Cut out the 4 corners of the Keel Beam as shown in **figure 4**. Then fold the Keel Beam in half along its centerline so that the reinforcement pieces are on the inside and the sides of the beam are spaced 3" apart as shown in **figure 6**.

In order to achieve an uninterrupted continuous bond between the bottom edges of the Keel Beam and the bottom of the hull, the bottom edges of the Keel Beam need to rest flat against the ground in order to rest flat against the bottom of the Hull.

Step 4: (See the Construction Note on page 42). As you squeeze the Keel Beam together in a triangular shape, place the bottom edges of the corrugated cardboard on a flat surface of asphalt or concrete. Press down firmly and rub the Keel Beam back and forth across the rough surface pressing down evenly during the process. This will shape the bottom edges of the cardboard flat against the asphalt or concrete surface. Continue to swipe the Keel Beam back and forth with even pressure until the entire length of the Keel Beam is flat.

Step 5: Apply contact cement to the bottom edges of the Keel Beam and the area on the bottom of the Hull where the Keel Beam makes contact with the Hull. See **photo 1**.

Step 6: Install the Keel Beam to the bottom of the Hull along the centerline of the Hull as shown in **figure 7 and photo 2**. Apply pressure along the entire length of the Keel Beam to ensure continuous and consistent contact is made.

Allow the bond between the Keel Beam and the Hull to cure before going to the next step.

Step 7: Hold a straightedge along the bottom of the Bow and along the side of the Keel Beam. Trim off the front of the Keel Beam following the angle of the Bow as shown in **figure 7**.

Step 8: Cut a small triangular shape of cardboard to cover both ends of the Keel Beam. Cement the triangular covers in place over both ends of the Keel Beam.

When you are done with this step your boat will look like **figure 7 and photo 2**.

DONE If you intend to install the Dent-Resistance material proceed to **Installing Dent-Resistance Material** on page 44, otherwise proceed to **Taping Your Kayaker** on page 46.

What is the purpose of the Keel Beam?

The Keel Beam serves two purposes. **1)** It maintains the directional stability of your boat by helping to keep it headed in the direction you are steering your boat. **2)** The Keel Beam is also an important structural strength component of your boat. When you sit in your boat you are sitting on top of the Keel Beam. The Keel Beam assists in transferring the force of your weight to the sides of the boat, the Compression Beam, and the Bulkhead. Because of this it is very important to achieve a strong and consistent bond between the Keel Beam and the bottom of your boat.

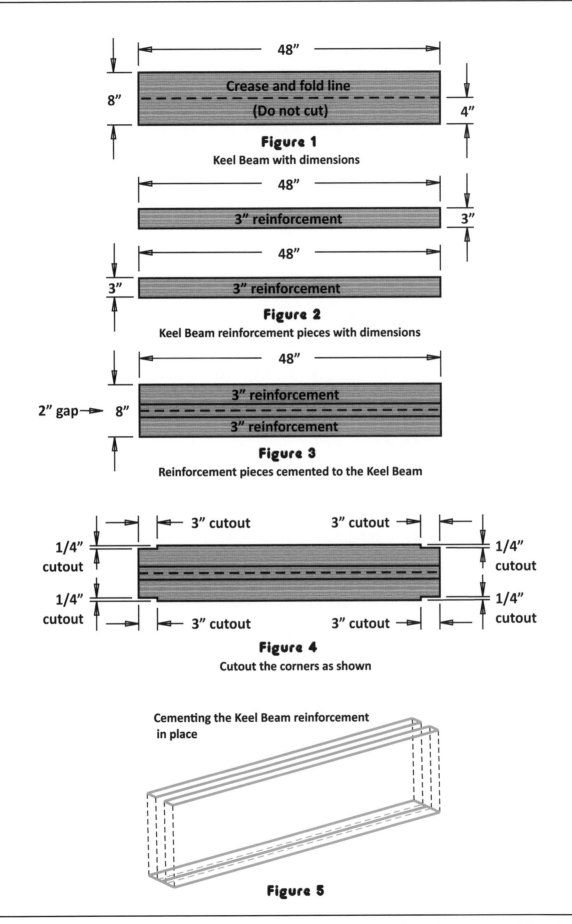

48"

8"

Crease and fold line
(Do not cut)

4"

Figure 1
Keel Beam with dimensions

48"

3" reinforcement

3"

48"

3"

3" reinforcement

Figure 2
Keel Beam reinforcement pieces with dimensions

48"

3" reinforcement

2" gap 8"

3" reinforcement

Figure 3
Reinforcement pieces cemented to the Keel Beam

3" cutout   3" cutout

1/4"
cutout

1/4"
cutout

1/4"
cutout

1/4"
cutout

3" cutout   3" cutout

Figure 4
Cutout the corners as shown

Cementing the Keel Beam reinforcement
in place

Figure 5

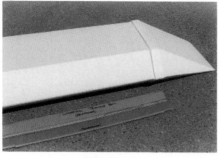

Photo 1

Preparing to cement the Keel Beam to the underside of the Hull.
Keel Beam cements over the Bow and Stern Tabs.

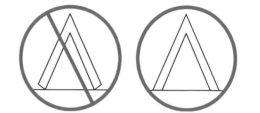

CONSTRUCTION NOTE: It is important to achieve a uniform and consistent bond between the Keel Beam and the bottom of the Hull along the entire length of the Beam and the entire thickness of the cardboard. Squeeze the Beam together until the sides are 3" apart and sand the edge of the Beam against a flat concrete or asphalt surface in order to ensure the cardboard is shaped flat against the ground and therefore will be flat against the bottom of the Hull when you cement the Beam to the Hull.

Photo 2

Center the Keel Beam along the centerline on the underside of the Hull. The ends of the Keel Beam cement over the Bow and Stern Tabs. Fold the Keel Beam 3" apart when cementing to the bottom of the Hull. Before cementing the Beam to the Hull, sand the Keel Beam flat against a cement or asphalt surface. This will flatten the edges of the Keel Beam that cement to the Hull to ensure a consistent and continuous bond between the Keel Beam and the Hull. See Construction Note.

1) After the Keel Beam is installed on the Hull cut the front of the Beam off at an angle inline with the bottom of the Bow

2) Cap both ends of the Keel Beam with cardboard after the Beam is installed

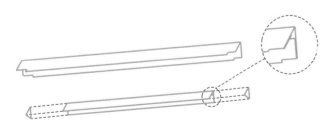

Figure 6

Shows the reinforcement inside the Keel Beam and the cutouts on the ends of the Keel Beam

Figure 7

Installing the Keel Beam

Installing Dent-Resistance Material

Intro You have the option of installing Dent-Resistance material on select edges of the boats exterior. The purpose of the Dent-Resistance material is to protect specific edges of the boat from premature damage due to normal use of your boat. Please note that the Dent-Resistance material is NOT REQUIRED to build a structurally sound boat.

The Dent-Resistance material is a standard drywall finishing product used to finish the outside edges of wall and ceiling drywall. It is known as 'drywall corner-bead'.

Drywall corner-bead is available from home improvement or hardware stores.

You will need 28-feet of 90-degree outside corner-bead to install on one Kayaker. Corner-bead is available in different lengths. The typical lengths you will want to purchase for this application are 8' and 10' sections. The common lengths you will use are 48" and 18". There are some 4"- 6" pieces that are installed on the ends of the Keel Beam.

Edges to Protect The recommended edges to install the corner-bead are identified in **figures 1 and 2.** A list of the recommended edges and the typical reason for installing the corner-bead on these edges are as follows.

• Top edge of the Hull: Protection from resting the paddle on the Kayaker.
• Front and Bottom edge of the Keel Beam: Protection from underwater obstacles.
• Top of the Compression Beam: Protection from users and equipment resting on the Compression Beam.

• Outside edges of the Hull: Protection from docks, piers, and rafting to other boats.
• Front and back of the Bow and Stern: Protection from docks, piers, and rafting to other boats.

There are reasons for not installing the Dent-Resistance material. For example, most organized cardboard boat events typically do not allow the use of this type of material. If you are building a Kayaker for an organized event please review the building material requirements prior to installing the Dent-Resistance material.

If you have chosen to install the Dent-Resistance material proceed to step 1 to begin the installation. Otherwise proceed to **Taping Your Kayaker** on page 46.

Step 1: Measure the length of material to cover an edge and cut the material with a metal hacksaw or other sheet-metal cutter.

NOTE: Some edges require the material to be installed at an angle smaller than 90-degrees to make positive contact with the edge. In this case carefully bend the material together as required to achieve consistent contact between the edge you are protecting and the Dent-Resistance material.

Step 2: Pre-fit the piece of material to the edge to be protected to ensure consistent contact before applying contact cement. Then, apply contact cement to the inside of the corner-bead and apply contact cement to the edge to be protected. Once the contact cement is dry press the corner-bead onto the edge.

Continue this process for each edge to be protected. Some corner-bead may also need to have tape applied over the ends to cover any exposed metal of the material.

Done Once you have completed installing the Dent-Resistance material on the edges identified by the color 'red' on **figures 1 and 2,** proceed to **Taping Your Kayaker**.

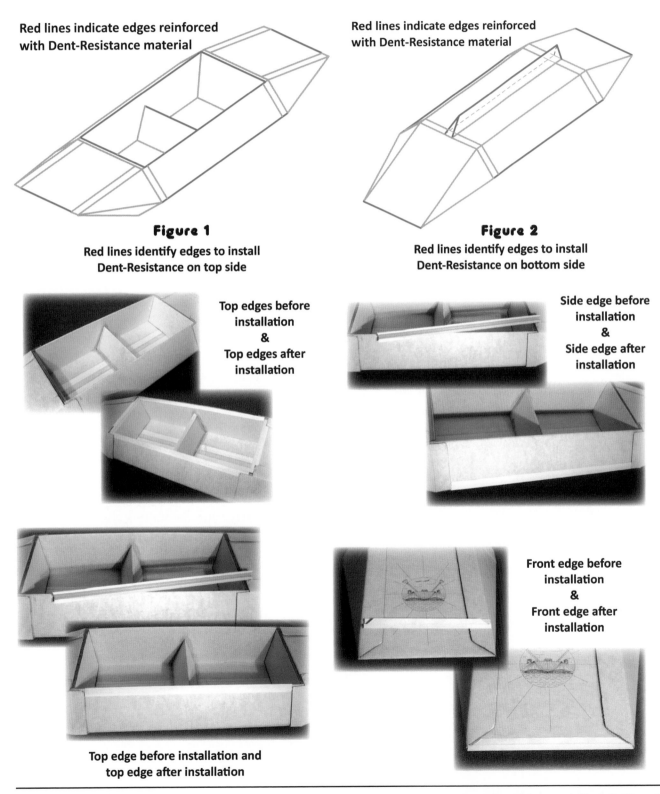

Red lines indicate edges reinforced
with Dent-Resistance material

Red lines indicate edges reinforced
with Dent-Resistance material

Figure 1
Red lines identify edges to install
Dent-Resistance on top side

Figure 2
Red lines identify edges to install
Dent-Resistance on bottom side

Top edges before
installation
&
Top edges after
installation

Side edge before
installation
&
Side edge after
installation

Front edge before
installation
&
Front edge after
installation

Top edge before installation and
top edge after installation

Taping Your Kayaker

Intro to Taping

The goal of taping is to seal every seam and edge that is a point of entry for water penetrating into the inner structure of your boat using paper drywall tape. All seams and edges that need to be taped are identified in **figures 1 and 2**. Use contact cement to adhere the paper drywall tape to the cardboard.

Your boat can last for many years if you are patient and meticulous and take your time taping your boat. You do not want to rush this step.

Contact Cement

There are many contact cement products on the market to choose from. In order to maintain the 'eco-friendly' claim of *The Cardboard Boat Book* you MUST use a contact cement product that meets the requirements and standards for being environmentally-friendly.

Products can be found at do-it-yourself home improvement stores or by searching the Internet for "Environmentally-friendly contact cement", or "Eco-Friendly contact cement".

NOTE: Eco-Friendly products are defined as being 'non-toxic' and having a 'low VOC content' (Volatile-Organic-Compound). They do not fill your work area with hazardous fumes and they are water-based as opposed to solvent-based. This type of contact cement is not hazardous to the environment.

Taping

The seams that need to be taped are identified with blue lines in **figures 1 and 2**. The process of taping is explained in the following steps.

If you have any question whether or not a seam or edge should be taped, tape it! Better to be safe than sorry when dealing with the potential of water damage.

Step 1:

Cut a piece of tape long enough to cover the seam or edge you are taping. Fold the tape in half along its centerline to allow the tape to fit into a corner or over an edge.

Place the tape on a scrap piece of cardboard to protect the area under the tape from being damaged by the contact cement.

Apply contact cement to the side of the tape that will be adhered to the boat and to both sides of the seam or edge you are taping.

Allow the contact cement to dry according to the manufacturer's recommendation.

Step 2:

Then, press the tape into the corner or onto the seam or edge. The goal is to achieve a close fit between the tape and the boat with no open space or air gaps between the tape and the cardboard.

Step 3:

Continue cutting pieces of tape to length and cementing the tape to each and every seam and exposed edge of cardboard identified in **figures 1 and 2**.

Refer to the photos for examples of the taping process.

Done

Once you are confident that all seams are properly taped, proceed to **Waterproofing Your Kayaker**.

Blue lines indicate seams between component parts and exposed cut edges of cardboard that must be taped in preparation for painting

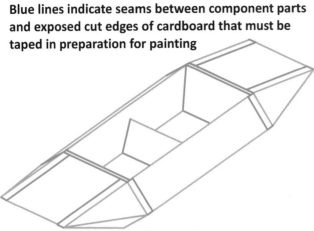

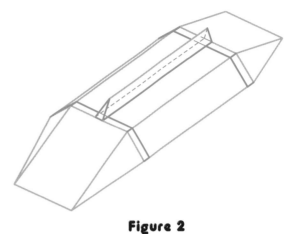

Figure 1
Blue lines identify seams to be taped on the top side

Figure 2
Blue lines identify seams to be taped on the bottom side

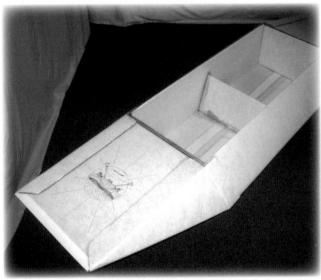

Kayaker before taping

Kayaker after taping

Hull with Dent-Resistance installed, fully taped, and ready for waterproofing

Bow before taping   Bow after taping

Compression Beam before taping   Compression Beam after taping

Bulkhead before taping   Bulkhead after taping

Stern before taping

Stern after taping

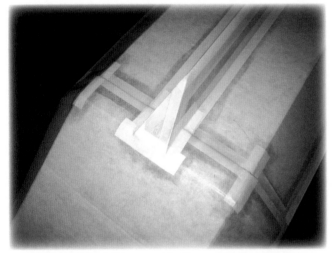

Front of Keel Beam and bottom of Hull and Bow

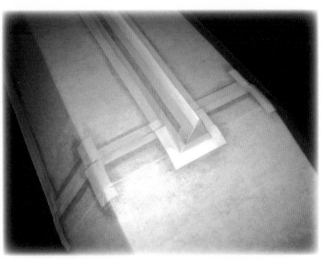

Rear of Keel Beam and bottom of Hull and Stern

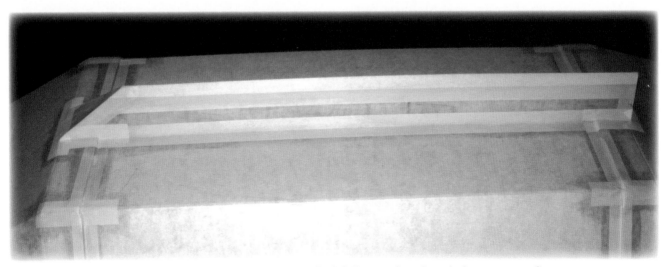

Keel Beam with Dent-Resistance installed, fully taped, and ready for waterproofing

Waterproofing Your Kayaker

Intro The process of waterproofing your boat consists of painting it inside and out with three coats of a waterproof coating.

Your boat can last many years if you maintain your waterproof coating.

Water Proof Product There are many waterproof coating products on the market to choose from. In order to comply with the eco-friendly claim of *The Cardboard Boat Book* you MUST use a waterproof coating product that meets the requirements and standards for being environmentally-friendly.

Products can be found at do-it-yourself home improvement stores or by searching the Internet for "Environmentally-friendly waterproof coating", or "Eco-Friendly waterproof coating".

NOTE: Eco-Friendly products are defined as being 'non-toxic' and having a 'low VOC content' (Volatile-Organic-Compound). These products will not fill your work area with hazardous fumes and they are water-based as opposed to solvent-based. This type of waterproof coating is not hazardous to the environment.

Step 1: Begin by turning your boat upside down so that the bottom of your boat is facing upwards.

Bottom Coat 1 Paint the entire bottom side of your boat with one complete coating. Allow to dry to the manufacturer's specifications.

Step 2: Turn your boat over so the top side is facing upwards.

Top Coat 1 Paint the entire top side of your boat inside and out with one complete coating. Allow to dry according to the manufacturer's recommendations.

Step 3: Turn your boat upside down so that the bottom side of your boat is facing upwards.

Bottom Coat 2 Paint the entire bottom side of your boat with one complete coating. Allow to dry to the manufacturer's specifications.

Step 4: Turn your boat over so the top side is facing upwards.

Top Coat 2 Paint the entire top side of your boat inside and out with one complete coating. Allow the material to dry to the manufacturer's specifications.

Step 5: Turn your boat upside down so that the bottom side of your boat is facing upwards.

Bottom Coat 3 Paint the entire bottom side of your boat with one complete coating. Allow to dry to the manufacturer's specifications.

Step 6: Turn your boat over so the top side is facing upwards.

Top Coat 3 Paint the entire top side of your boat inside and out with one complete coating. Allow the material to dry to the manufacturer's specifications.

Your boat has received a satisfactory waterproof coating after three (3) coats of the waterproof material has been applied to both the top and the bottom sides of your boat.

DONE The construction of your Kayaker is now complete and it is ready for a water test.

Safety Before placing your boat in the water for the first time read the safety recommendations on page 50.

Always wear an approved Personal-Flotation-Device (PFD) when in and around water.

A trio of cardboard boats in a two-tone color scheme. A light brown coating on top and a dark brown coating on the bottom.
(Left - The ORIGINAL Kayaker; Middle - The 'Tippy' Canoe; Right - The Tri-Maran)

The tips provided on this page are intended to provide you with 'best-practices' recommendations for safely enjoying your boat. These recommendations have been developed during many hours of cardboard boating. The recommendations may seem obvious to many but the intent is to ensure everyone's safety while spending time in a cardboard boat.

Whatever you choose to do always observe the global recommendation of using a Personal-Flotation-Device (PFD) whenever you are in or around water. This recommendation applies to spending time in a cardboard boat.

What NOT to do with a Cardboard Boat

DO NOT try to stand up in your boat. Cardboard Boats should be treated like any Kayak or Canoe and may tip over if you try to stand up in it.

DO NOT try to get into your boat from the shore or shallow water. The bottom of your boat may scrape the bottom of the lake and get roughed up if you try this.

DO NOT use a Cardboard Boat without wearing an approved Personal-Flotation-Device (PFD) that is properly rated for you.

DO NOT use a Cardboard Boat in swift moving rivers or rivers of any kind. Leave this type of activity to boats that have been specifically designed to be used in rivers.

DO NOT use a Cardboard Boat in lakes with rough water or white caps unless you have experience with this type of water condition.

DO NOT use a Cardboard Boat without the skill and experience to properly maneuver and propel the boat.

DO NOT use a Cardboard Boat without competent people supervising your activity.

DO NOT leave your boat in direct sunlight when it is out of the water. The cardboard will expand and unattractive creases can appear.

How to use a Cardboard Boat safely

Purchase a Kayak style double-ended paddle to maneuver and propel your Cardboard Boat. Inexpensive Kayak paddles can be purchased from most sporting goods stores.

Sit in your Cardboard Boat leaning slightly forward with your knees over the Compression Beam and your feet in the front compartment.

Leaning forward in your boat lowers your center of gravity and provides for the most stable ride when you are operating your boat in rough water or when paddling through large waves.

Make a habit of checking your boat for structural or water damage any time you believe your boat may have contacted something under water.

Always wear a Personal-Flotation-Device (PFD) that is properly rated for you.

The safest way to get in and out of your Cardboard Boat

The sequence of photos 1 through 5 on the next page depicts how to get in and out of your boat in the best and safest manner possible.

Photo 1: Place your boat in the water next to a dock. You will have the best experience if the dock is no more than 6-inches above the top of the boat. Sit on the edge of the dock and place your feet in the front compartment of the boat.

Photo 2: While holding onto the dock for stability lower yourself into the boat and rest yourself lightly on the Compression Beam.

Photo 3: While holding onto the dock with one hand place your other hand on the top edge of your boat and lower yourself into the rear compartment of the boat.

Photo 4: Situate yourself comfortably in your boat.

Photo 5: Grab your paddle and you are ready to go!

When you return from boating reverse the above procedure to get out of your boat.

Photo 1
Sit on the dock and put your feet in your boat

Leaning forward when operating your boat in rough water lowers your center of gravity and stabilizes your ride

Photo 2
While holding the dock lower yourself into your boat

Photo 3
Holding the dock and your boat slide into position

Photo 4
Get yourself situated

Photo 5
Ready to go!

Transporting Your Kayaker

Cardboard Boats can be carried inside an automobile, and on top of an automobile.

Whichever way you transport your boat follow the tips outlined below.

Place protective material over any edge of your boat that will make contact with other surfaces. Surfaces that the boat may come in contact with can be a roof top carrier or the edges of a tailgate in a car or SUV.

Recommended material to protect your boat with is bubble wrap, pieces of cardboard, or pressed paperboard used to protect shipping containers from damage.

The goal is to protect any edge of your boat that could be subject to being damaged during transport.

Storing Your Kayaker

Storing your boat indoors in a dry heated area is highly recommended. To protect your boat place a piece of cardboard under any part of the boat that will touch the ground.

Accessorizing Your Cardboard Boat

There are a few accessories that are very useful and add value to your boating experience.

Install an inexpensive padded car seat cover in the rear compartment of the boat where you sit. This is highly recommended to provide a comfortable boating experience.

Install a beverage holder on the inside of the boat against the front Bulkhead. Many inexpensive plastic holders are available at boating supply and sporting goods stores.

Repairing and Caring for Your Cardboard Boat

Regularly examine your boat for water damage. If you locate any soft spots on your boat place your boat in a warm and dry location and allow it to thoroughly dry. This can take up to 2-weeks or more if the damage is a large area.

Once your boat has dried so the cardboard is firm again locate any visible hole or crack in the cardboard. Cement a piece of paper drywall tape over the affected area. Paint the area with 3 layers of your waterproof coating and allow to dry per the manufacturer's recommendations.

In extreme cases of damage you can cut out the affected area with a razor knife and replace it with a new piece of cardboard. Thoroughly tape any patch you make with the paper wallboard tape and paint 3 layers of waterproof coating over the entire affected area.

Some of my Cardboard Boats have been in regular use for over 22 years and are still being used. This is testament to the fact that if you take care of your cardboard boat it can last for a long time.

Appendix 1: 2-Piece Hull Layout

The instructions listed in this Appendix provide an option for building the Hull with 2-pieces of cardboard instead of the 1-piece construction described in the main building instructions. Follow these instructions to **Step 9** and then return to **Step 7** of the main building instructions to continue building your Kayaker.

Step 1: Lay two 43-3/4" x 48" cardboard sheets out flat on the floor. Place the 43-3/4" lengths together as shown. The corrugation flutes must run the 48" width of the sheets.

Step 2: Cut a 6" x 46" splice piece to size. Cement the splice piece to the 2-sheets in order to cement them together as shown in **figure 1.**

You now have one large sheet 48" wide by 87-1/2" long.

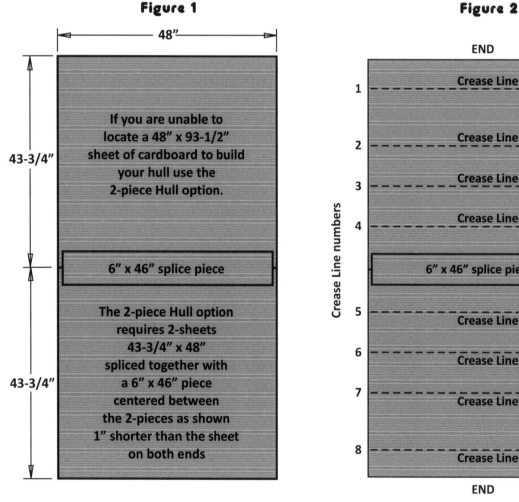

Splice the Hull pieces together

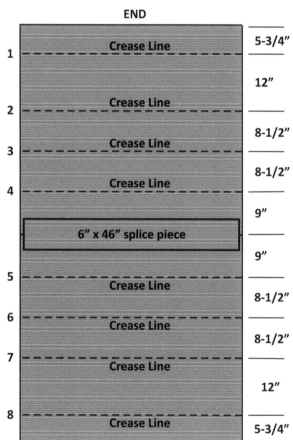

Measure and draw the crease lines

Step 3: Working from the splice line of the 2-sheets, measure and draw the crease-lines as shown in **figure 2** towards both ends of the sheet. Number the crease-lines as you draw them as shown on **figure 2**. When you have completed this step there should be 8 crease-lines on the sheet.

Step 4: The area between the 8 crease-lines are referred to as panels. There are 9 panels on the sheet. The center panel, #5, has two halves, labeled 5a and 5b, on either side of the splice. Number the panels as shown on **figure 3**.

Step 5: Cut the 1"-wide by 2-panel long strip of cardboard from each corner of the Hull sheet as shown in **figure 4**. (This cutout will accommodate the Bulkheads).

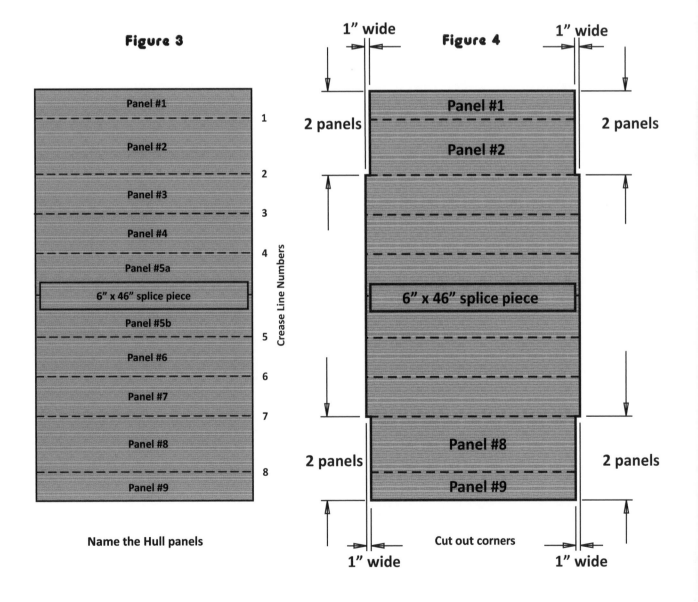

Step 6: Measure and cut the 4 Hull reinforcement panels to shape. (2 panels measure 10" x 46" and 2 panels measure 11" x 46").

Step 7: Cement the 11" wide reinforcement panels to the center of Hull panels 2 and 8 as shown in **Figure 5**.

Step 8: Cement the 10" wide reinforcement panels to the center of the 11" wide panels as shown in **Figure 5**.

Crease the 8 crease-lines in preparation for folding the Hull into shape. (**Note:** Panels 1 & 9 fold away from the sheet. Crease-lines 1 and 8 should be creased on the opposite side of the sheet.) When you are done reinforcing the Hull your sheet should look like **Figure 6**.

Step 9: Return to Step 7 of the **Hull Construction** instructions on page 16 to continue building the Hull.

Figure 5

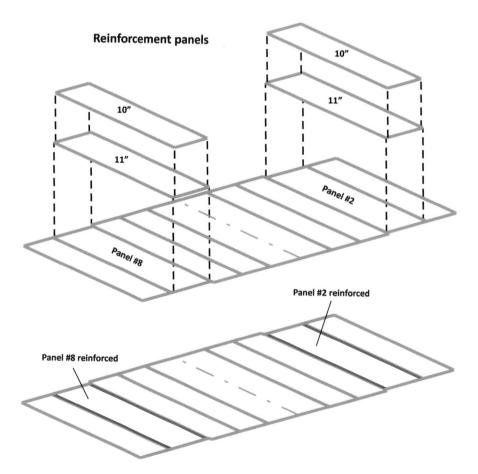

Installing the Hull reinforcement
• Cement the 11" wide panels to panel #2 & #8.
•Cement the 10" wide panels to the 11" wide panels.

Figure 6

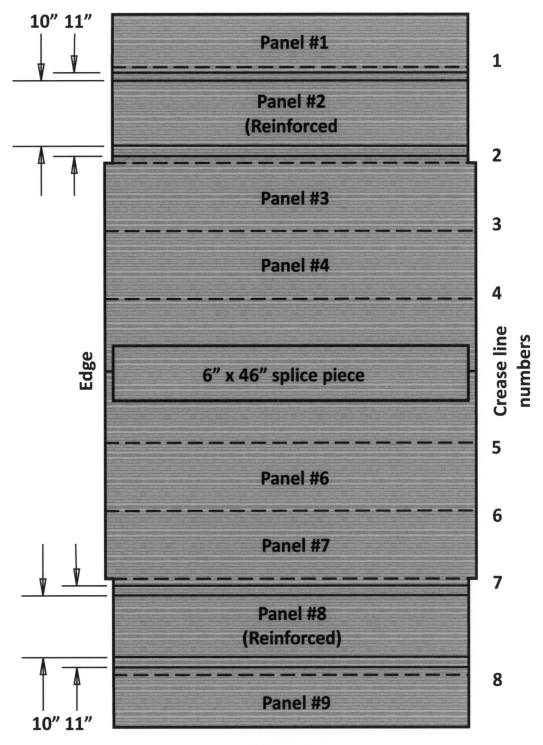

10" 11"

Panel #1

1

Panel #2
(Reinforced

2

Panel #3

3

Panel #4

4

Edge

6" x 46" splice piece

Crease line numbers

5

Panel #6

6

Panel #7

7

10" 11"

Panel #8
(Reinforced)

8

10" 11"

Panel #9

Finished Hull layout with
reinforcement installed

     The Cardboard Boat Book

Appendix 2: FAQs

Do people really use cardboard boats?

You bet they do! Annual cardboard boat regattas attract thousands of spectators and hundreds of participants from around the United States. Check out some of the many links to cardboard boats on the web by searching for 'Cardboard Boats', 'Cardboard Boat Races', and/or 'Cardboard Boat Regattas'.

As of this writing I have not found an all paper corrugated-cardboard boat that is strong enough and water-resistant enough to be used over and over again like the boats in *The Cardboard Boat Book*. The boats in *The Cardboard Boat Book* have been in productive use since 1983!

NOTE: If you intend to participate in an organized cardboard boat race or sponsored regatta review the boat design specifications and requirements for the event to verify that you can enter with one of the boats in *The Cardboard Boat Book*. The boats in *The Cardboard Boat Book* typically EXCEED the design specifications for many organized cardboard boat events.

Can you explain how the boats are protected from water damage?

The construction process includes covering and sealing all exposed edges of cardboard with non-adhesive paper drywall tape adhered with contact cement to completely seal the boat from water entering inside the cardboard.

Once the boat is fully taped, the boat is painted with a waterproof coating. When the taping and coating is properly done the cardboard is protected from water damage. We have boats that are over 22 years old and are still being used!

What type of coating do you recommend to provide maximum water protection?

We recommend a waterproof coating formulated for outdoor wood or concrete structures. (Please note that waterproof coatings are different than waterproof paints.)

Waterproof coatings can sometimes be found at lumber yards and hardware stores. They are not typically found at 'do-it-yourself' home improvement stores.

Coatings that we have had good success with are manufactured by Ames Research and Consolidated Coatings.

If I puncture a hole in my boat how do I repair it?

If you puncture a hole in your boat we advise you to immediately remove the boat from water and allow it to completely dry. This can take two or more weeks if the damaged area is large.

Once the cardboard is completely dry and firm we recommend patching the area with paper drywall tape and contact cement, the same material that you constructed your boat with. Once the contact cement is completely cured you can coat the affected area with the waterproof coating.

NOTE: Use non-sticky paper drywall tape and adhere the tape to your boat with contact cement. DO NOT USE self-adhesive drywall tape. You will not achieve satisfactory results.

Can you explain what cardboard is and the history behind cardboard?

A good source for learning about cardboard can be found in the online free encyclopedia, Wikipedia.

Where do I find cardboard to build a boat?

Many large appliances and large pieces of furniture are shipped in 275# test, 1/4 inch thick, double-wall corrugated cardboard boxes. These boxes can be used to build a boat. Check with your local appliance and furniture outlets for these types of cardboard boxes.

New sheets of 275# test, 1/4 inch thick, double-wall corrugated cardboard can be located on the web by searching for 'cardboard sheets', 'corrugated sheets', or 'corrugated packaging'.

If I have all of the materials to build a boat how long will it take to build?

With two people working together we have measured and cut out the 21-pieces of cardboard, constructed all of the component parts, and assembled a boat in one day, including taping the boat. Once assembled and taped, the contact cement is allowed to cure. (The contact cement is cured when you cannot detect a strong odor. This typically takes 12 hours.)

Once the contact cement is cured the boats are coated inside and out with a minimum of three (3) coats of waterproof coating. If the coatings are applied in succession, leaving time for each coat to fully cure, it is reasonable to expect that you can have a boat ready to place in the water within 7 days from the start of construction.

What type of paddles or oars do you recommend?

We recommend Kayak style oars with paddles on both ends. Inexpensive Kayak oars can be found at many sporting goods stores. Sources for Kayak oars can be located on the web by searching for 'Kayak oars' or 'Kayak paddles'.

Can I use my boat in salt water?

We HAVE NOT tested the cardboard boats in salt water and therefore do not have any advice on this matter. We recommend that you use your boat in fresh water lakes only.

Can I take my cardboard boat white water rafting on a river?

NO! We highly discourage this activity. Leave this activity for boats that have been specifically built for white water rafting.

When on the water always wear a Coast Guard approved Personal-Flotation-Device (PFD).

Boat smart from the start! Wear a life jacket!

Learn all about being safe on the water at the "National Safe Boating Council".

Appendix 3: Web Resources

The information in this Appendix is intended to assist you in locating the materials, products, and tools required to build a cardboard boat.

Also provided is assistance on how to locate information on cardboard boats on the web. There are a large number of people and organizations that hold annual cardboard boat events throughout the world. You only need to spend a short amount of time on the Internet to learn how many people are involved in the sport of cardboard boating.

Cardboard on the Web
Search for 'Cardboard Sheets'
Search for 'Corrugated Sheets'
Search for '275 lb. test Corrugated Sheets'
Search for 'Corrugated Packing Material'

Local Sources for Cardboard Sheets
New cardboard sheets can be found at some Home Improvement stores.
Look in your local Yellow Pages for 'Corrugated Packing Material' or 'Corrugated Sheets'. 48" x 96" and 60" x 120" are standard size sheets.

Eco-Friendly Products on the Web
Search for 'Environmentally-Friendly Contact Cement'
Search for 'Eco-Friendly Contact Cement'
Search for 'Titan DX Premium Contact Cement'
Search for 'AmesResearch' - Waterproof coatings
Search for 'Deckote' - Waterproof Coatings

Tools and Accessories on the Web
Search for 'Beam Compass'. There are a number of designs you can build with minimal materials.
Search for 'Car Seat Covers' or 'Car Seat Pads' or 'Car Seat Cushions'.

Local Sources for Accessories
Check your local automobile supply stores for car seat cushions.
Check your local sporting goods stores for seat cushions.
Check your local sporting goods stores for beverage holders.
Check your local sporting goods stores for Personal Floatation Devices

Cardboard Boats on the Web
Search for 'Cardboard Boats'
Search for 'The Cardboard Boat Book'
Search for 'Cardboard Boat Events'
Search for 'Cardboard Boat Races'
Search for 'Cardboard Boat Regattas'

Ready for Fishing!
Shown is a PFD and car Seat Cushion

3520241R00051

Printed in Germany
by Amazon Distribution
GmbH, Leipzig